AF614895

Praise for *The Rule*

"Men need a code to live by. With simplicity, directness, and insightful wisdom, *The Rule* gives men solid counsels to become like St. Joseph — the son, husband, and father that God is calling them to be. I highly recommend this spiritual treasure to any man who is serious about becoming a saint."

— Fr. Donald Calloway, M.I.C., Author, *Consecration to St. Joseph*

"Devin's personal battles, failings, trials, and triumphs as a husband, father, and son of God have provided us the timeless wisdom contained in *The Rule*. Men, young and old, preparing for marriage and already married, will benefit greatly from this treasure."

— Matt Fradd, Creator and Host, *Pints with Aquinas*

"Every man wants to fulfill his God-given mission as the guardian of his family and of the dignity of womanhood. However, few are offered a concrete plan for how to execute this calling. They're told to be 'spiritual leaders' but without a clear picture of what this means or how to be one. *The Rule* fills this niche, offering daily reflections that are concise and profound. This manual will be a blessing for all men who read it — and, in turn, for all those whom God has entrusted to them."

— Jason Evert, Founder, Chastity Project

"In the heart of every man is a desire for greatness, the kind of greatness that lasts forever. No man sets out to be mediocre. The problem is, most of us have no clear path forward. *The Rule* is a comprehensive and powerful guide for every man to become who God created him to be. It's more than a manual — it's a light in the darkness.

"Rooted in the example of St. Joseph, this book gives men real direction, not fluff. It's honest, practical, and spiritually solid. Every page calls you higher — not through guilt or hype but through a clear vision of who you are as a son of God, a husband, and a father. Devin has lived this. He has wrestled with the same battles we all face, and what he offers here is hard-won, practical wisdom and spiritual insights.

I wish I had had this book when I was starting out. I recommend this to every man and every father. Even for those who seem to 'have it together,' this book will serve as a wellspring of inspiration."

— Gabriel Castillo, Catholic Evangelist; Author; Founder, True Faith TV

"You can tell when a man has battled and prayed to live out his vocation as a beloved son of the Father, a self-giving bridegroom like Jesus, and a faithful father like St. Joseph. This is true of Devin Schadt. The wisdom gained from his trust in God and the Church is evident in every page of *The Rule*. I highly recommend this book to every man — young and old alike. It is a blueprint for being a man after God's own heart!"

— Dr. Bob Schuchts, Founder, John Paul II Healing Center; Co-host, *Restore the Glory* podcast

"*The Rule* is the most powerful, direct, and focused guide for fathers that I've ever encountered — one that leads them to discover and embrace their sacred role as guardians of their families.

"We live in an age in which the loudest and most divisive voices dominate the stage. Men are left disoriented, grabbing onto whatever sounds good, yet lacking a true and lasting power source when real-life trials hit. *The Rule* offers a profound reset. It delivers the framework that we have yet to see for men today: clear, grounded, and refreshingly ordered and easy to follow. It cuts through the noise of modern life and reconnects men to the divine call of fatherhood, as modeled by St. Joseph.

"I strongly urge all men to grab this book, take it to prayer, and reflect deeply on the wisdom it contains. Devin Schadt writes from authentic experience, having weathered the burdens, sufferings, and sacrifices of life while finding joy and unwavering hope. It's from this balanced perspective — grounded in both life's trials and its God-given blessings — that he offers practical guidance to share with all men.

"In a culture that has lost sight of true masculine fatherhood, *The Rule* illuminates the path forward with St. Joseph as our exemplar, offering not just theory but a practical rule of life that transforms confusion into purpose and strengthens a father's mission in life. Most importantly, this book reconnects men to their true power source: our God-given identity as sons of the Father and the transformative grace that flows from that relationship."

— John Heinen, Owner and Executive Director,
The Catholic Gentleman

"Men need structure and (whether or not they like to admit it) to be told what to do and why they need to do it. In this challenging yet straightforward book, Devin gives his readers the tools to embrace their ultimate calling as husbands and fathers through practical instruction and biblical wisdom. I wish I'd had something this good as a young father!"

— Keith Nester, Executive Director, Down to Earth Ministries

"Devin Schadt understands the male psyche and soul. He is able to penetrate the deepest needs of men, coaching them and equipping them with the strength, authority, and confidence they need to achieve their mission as husbands, fathers, and men of God."

— Timmerie Geagea, Host,
Relevant Radio's *Trending with Timmerie*

The Rule

Counsels and Directives for Husbands and Fathers

Devin Schadt

SOPHIA INSTITUTE PRESS
Manchester, New Hampshire

Cover and interior design by Devin Schadt.

Sophia Institute Press
Box 5284, Manchester, NH 03108
1-800-888-9344
www.SophiaInstitute.com

leatherette ISBN 979-8-88911-538-0

ebook ISBN 979-8-88911-539-7

Library of Congress Control Number: 2025938953

First printing

To Chris.

You believed in me even perhaps when I lost belief in myself. You imparted to me God's strength and confidence, that I may impart His strength and confidence to others. As you encouraged me to persist in this work, may this work be an encouragement to men to persevere in their noble calling. I am deeply grateful for you.

"The essence and role of the family are in the final analysis specified by love. Hence the family has the mission to guard, reveal and communicate love, and this is a living reflection of and a real sharing in God's love for humanity and the love of Christ the Lord for the Church his bride." This being the case, it is in the Holy Family, the original "Church in miniature (Ecclesia domestica)," that every Christian family must be reflected. "Through God's mysterious design, it was in that family that the Son of God spent long years of a hidden life. It is therefore the prototype and example for all Christian families."

—St. Pope John Paul II, *Redemptoris Custos* 7

St. Joseph was called by God to serve the person and mission of Jesus directly through the exercise of his fatherhood. It is precisely in this way that, as the Church's Liturgy teaches, he "cooperated in the fullness of time in the great mystery of salvation" and is truly a "minister of salvation." His fatherhood is expressed concretely "in his having made his life a service, a sacrifice to the mystery of the Incarnation and to the redemptive mission connected with it; in having used the legal authority which was his over the Holy Family in order to make a total gift of self, of his life and work; in having turned his human vocation to domestic love into a superhuman oblation of self, an oblation of his heart and all his abilities into love placed at the service of the Messiah growing up in his house."

—St. Pope John Paul II, *Redemptoris Custos* 8

Contents

Preface

One of the largest segments of the Body of Christ is fathers. Because it is so large, there is a great need for these Christian men to be formed in the ways of Jesus Christ specific to their noble vocation. Society goes by way of the family, and the family goes by way of the father. Therefore, it is imperative that the Church make every effort to provide this constituency with the spiritual formation necessary to fulfill this most important and heroic calling. The Church, in her vast depth and universality, has, by the grace of God — and due to the distinct spiritual needs of individuals throughout the ages — developed an array of spiritualities that uniquely guide and direct Christians in their calling to be disciples of Jesus Christ, toward communion with God the Father by the working of the Holy Spirit. Demonic adversarial challenges, particularly the relentless assault on marriage and the family, demands that, in this age, a spirituality for fathers be articulated, proclaimed, and lived, with the great hope that the Body of Christ may experience a renewal of faith, strength, and vitality in the Holy Spirit.

As the founder of the Fathers of St. Joseph and co-host on *The Catholic Gentleman*, I believe that part of my God-given calling in this life is to do all in my power to transmit this spirituality to the men of our age. St. Joseph is the starting point for all of this. He is the exemplar of husbands and the model for all fathers. In his example, we discover a spirituality that has the mark of masculine simplicity and order as well as profound depth and insight. Several popes and Doctors of the Church have referred to him as the *Custos*, a Latin word that means *keeper, custodian*, or *guard*. St. Joseph's spirituality is founded upon the four pillars that upheld him throughout his life in his dual role of heroic husband and faithful father: embrace silence, embrace woman, embrace the child, and embrace charitable authority. In his embrace of silence, he received confirmation of his noble identity, and thus he received his vocation, his mission: to embrace the Woman, the Most Blessed Virgin Mary as his own and, by receiving her, to embrace God's Son as his very own. God endowed St. Joseph with the fatherly authority and headship necessary to fulfill this superhuman vocation. These are the pillars that constitute the spirituality of the Custos.

It has been the effort of my adult life to determine a manner by which these four pillars, in their simplicity, can be articulated with clarity and precision so as to afford every man the means to fulfill his calling to be like St. Joseph — a human icon of God the Father and a man who images the Bridegroom Jesus Christ. To that end, this book outlines specific rules and corresponding spiritual practices that apply St. Joseph's four pillars to daily life, demonstrating how men of our age can live them. Additionally, it provides counsels regarding divine sonship, counsels regarding embracing one's vocation, and counsels regarding work. The overall aim of these seven sections is to constitute the rule for the spirituality of husbands and fathers with precision and clarity.

It is my sincere hope that men worldwide embrace, be formed by, and live out this rule, not only individually but within small groups, wherein each rule can be discussed and expounded upon at length with the sincere intention to "be perfect, as your heavenly Father is perfect" (Matt. 5:48).

How to Use *The Rule*

The Rule, though profound and spiritually rich, can be deceptively concise and simple. Because of each rule's brevity, you may be tempted to read a rule hastily and proceed to the next, consuming a multitude of them in one sitting. Each rule and its associated spiritual practice, however, are intended to be used as tools of counsel and discernment, to be meditated on at length and applied to your life gradually. For this reason, it is recommended that the reader meditate upon one rule each day, striving to reflect on its implications in your life and your relationships, while also persevering to implement that rule's associated spiritual practice.

Often, it is the case that a man desirous of applying these counsels to his life will read the same counsel repeatedly for several days while attempting to apply that directive to his life.

Another effective way to use *The Rule* is to select one of the seven sections that the spirituality of the Custos comprises — for example, a man may select the section regarding marriage — and read all of the rules pertaining to that section in one or two sittings. This enables the reader to grasp the theme, vision, and intent of the section. Then, over the course of the following days, you can read one rule from that particular section each day while applying the associated spiritual practices to his life.

The Rule is not a "one and done" resource; rather, it has been created with the intention of being a lifelong spiritual companion — one that you can pray over with intentionality and at length, with a heartfelt desire for conversion and transformation.

You may bring *The Rule* with you to reflect upon during Holy Hours, to read and meditate upon before and after the Holy Sacrifice of the Mass, as a way to examine your conscience prior to the Sacrament of Confession, as a resource to aid you in your daily mental prayer, or as a travel companion when you are away from your domestic church.

Regard *The Rule* as your trusted companion to aid you in your discernment of God's motions, to identify when evil is at hand, and to know how to proceed on the path toward sanctity.

May our beloved patron, St. Joseph, be your trustworthy mentor and guide as you make every attempt to walk in his spiritual footsteps.

Ite ad Joseph!

Devin Schadt
October 13, 2022
Anniversary of St. Joseph's Appearance at Fátima

Section 1

Counsels Pertaining to Sonship

Rule 1

The Foundation of the Custos' Life and Mission

Let the Custos understand that his entire vocation — and in fact, his entire life — and his very salvation depend upon his believing, receiving, embracing, and trusting that God is his Father and that he is God's son in the Son of God; that God has chosen him for His own; that God loves him for who he is and not for what he has done or will do; and that God wills to perfect him in His love. The foundation of the Custos' mission is his identity as a trusting son of God the Father. By trusting that God is his Father and that His love is all-sufficient, he will become capable of enduring life's storms and tempests without falling prey to doubting the goodness of God. The Custos understands that all tests are allowed by God for the purpose of strengthening his trust in God his Father and for securing this filial trust deeply and permanently. This identity — the trusting son of God the Father — when embraced and well lived, will enable the Custos to be drawn by God and to draw others to God and to his and their ultimate destiny: union with the Most Blessed Trinity for all eternity.

Spiritual Practice

The Daily Prayer of Surrender to God the Father

Begin each morning first by kneeling, second by placing yourself in the holy presence of God the Father, and third by offering yourself to Him.

> *Father, I believe that You have chosen me and desire me for Yourself. I surrender all that I am and have to You. Do with me what You will. Whatever You do, I thank You, and I trust You. Let Your holy will be accomplished in me. I am totally Yours.*

Rule 2

The Source of the Power to Empty Oneself in Service to Others

Let the Custos understand that only the son who trusts that God is his loving Father and that His love is all-sufficient becomes capable of emptying himself of vain ambitions and of the desire to seek human honor and to cling to status and human glory. While walking away from these empty pursuits, he simultaneously becomes a servant to others, obediently embracing the Cross of Jesus Christ. The holy apostle says, "Have this mind among yourselves, which was in Christ Jesus, who, though he was in the form of God, did not count equality with God a thing to be grasped, but emptied himself, taking the form of a servant, being born in the likeness of men. And being found in human form he humbled himself and became obedient unto death, even death on a cross" (Phil. 2:5–8). The Word, God the Son, was capable of emptying Himself of being God alone; He became incarnate because of His trust that God His Father's love is all-sufficient. As the Carmelite Doctor says, "Nothing is lacking for those who have God; God alone is sufficient."[1] When the Custos believes and trusts in God the Father's love for him, he will not cling to human glory, nor seek human honors, for he knows and believes that God's love is never lacking. However, sadness that arises when human honors are not forthcoming, anxiousness about gaining recognition, and avoiding or resisting hidden acts of service to others are all signs that the evil spirits are influencing the Custos.

[1] Prayer of St. Teresa of Ávila, also known as her "Bookmark."

For it was Christ who said, "I do not receive glory from men" (John 5:41). This is a definitive statement of one who knows and trusts in His identity as the Son of God and believes and trusts in God the Father and His all-sufficient love for Him. Likewise, the true son of God, by believing in and embracing his identity, overcomes the temptation to usurp God's glory while also becoming capable of emptying himself for others. He knows and believes that, as he glorifies God, he will eventually be glorified in Him.

Spiritual Practice

Intentionally Recommit to Trusting in God the Father

The essence of divine sonship is trust in God the Father. Identify those aspects of your life that cause you fear, anxiety, depression, anger, frustration, and doubt in God's goodness. You will discover that underlying each of these sentiments is a lack of trust in God.

Throughout your day, whenever you encounter these doubts, first, pause and recognize God's presence in you, and second, recommit yourself to the Father by praying:

> *Abba, Father, I trust that You can do all things, even in me, a sinner.*

Rule 3

The Nature of Tests and the Intentions of the Evil Spirits During Such Trials

Let the Custos be aware that when encountering tests, trials, tribulations, sufferings, and setbacks, the evil spirits will gravely tempt him to doubt the goodness of the Fatherhood of God and to believe that God is distant, that God is the cause of his sufferings, that God is his enemy, and that God is not trustworthy. Doubt in God is the greatest insult against His divine benevolence, and therefore, the evil spirits derive the most heinous pleasure by instilling doubt into the soul of the Custos. As Our Lord Jesus disclosed to the saint of His divine mercy, "Why are you so fearful and why do you tremble when you are united to Me? I am displeased when a soul yields to vain terrors. Who will dare touch you when you are with Me? Most dear to Me is the soul who strongly believes in My goodness and has complete trust in Me. I heap my confidence upon that soul and give it all it asks."[2] Therefore, let the Custos understand that, as the Holy Spirit drove Jesus into the desert to be tested, it is God who leads the Custos into tests to perfect his trust. Again, as the evil one tempted Jesus to prove His worth and to bow down to the ways of the world, the flesh, and the devil, so also it is the evil one who intends to break the Custos' trust in God the Father during the test. The evil spirits attempt to break the Custos' trust by inducing doubt in his soul in hopes that the Custos will become self-reliant, attempt to prove his own worth, and attempt to obtain validation

[2] St. Faustina Kowalska, *Diary: Divine Mercy in My Soul*, no. 453.

from the world, or to surrender his pursuit of sanctity. Let the Custos be aware that the evil spirits instill doubt in the soul of man to restrain him from emptying himself for others, preventing him from enabling the revelation of the glory of God through man.

✝

Spiritual Practice

Sacred Meeting with God the Father

Many men are ineffective in changing the world for the better, living a fulfilled life, and winning souls for God because they fail to meet with God daily.

First, identify the time of day in which you can remain in God's presence without interruption. Second, during this time, ask God to reveal to you your "vain terrors." Third, surrender those fears and doubts to God the Father. If you wish to be intentional about this, you can, for example, pray in one of the following two ways:

> *In the name of Jesus, I surrender the vain terror of losing my job. Father, I trust in You.*
>
> *In the name of Jesus, I surrender the vain terror that You do not love me. Father, I trust in You.*

Rule 4

The Temptation of Seeking Human Glory

Let the Custos be aware that the evil spirits are bent on conditioning him to seek honors, validation, glory, and affirmation from men. If the Custos seeks the glory of men, he becomes incapable of glorifying God, for he is determined to glorify himself. If the Custos is determined to please men, he becomes incapable of pleasing God. As the holy apostle warns, "Do you know not that friendship with the world is enmity with God? Therefore whoever wishes to be a friend of the world makes himself an enemy of God" (James 4:4); and as another holy apostle says, "Am I now seeking the favor of men, or of God? Or am I trying to please men? If I were still pleasing men, I should not be a servant of Christ" (Gal. 1:10). Therefore, let the Custos understand that as the devil tempted Jesus to bow down to him in order to receive the kingdoms of the world, so also the evil spirits will tempt the Custos to bow down to the glory of men and so deter him from rendering glory unto God.

Spiritual Practice

Responding to Temptation of Vainglory

When you encounter the temptation to be jealous or envious or to seek recognition for a personal achievement, first, turn your attention to God; second, thank God for the talents and gifts He has given to the other (or to you); and third, pray:

O Lord, not to us, but to Your name be the glory.

Section 2

Counsels Pertaining to the Custos' Vocation

Rule 1

The Irrevocable Nature of the Custos' Vocation

Let the Custos be aware that by sacramentally vowing himself in lifelong fidelity to his wife, and by swearing before God to receive and raise children to God, he has irrevocably embraced his vocation as a husband and father as his primary path to holiness, glory, and union with God; therefore, he must not look for another primary path.

When a person sets out toward a destination, he selects his route and, once embarked, does not return to his point of origin to select an alternate route for the purpose of beginning again. In a similar manner, once a man has consecrated himself as a husband to his wife, he cannot return to a moment preceding this act of consecration and select another vocation. For as the psalmist decrees, "I am bound by the vows I made" (Ps. 56:12); and as the holy apostle says, "The gifts and call of God are irrevocable" (Rom. 11:29). Therefore, being a husband in the image of Christ and a father in the image of God the Father is the Custos' primary vocational path to attain union with God and to glorify Him. All other paths to holiness are subsequent, secondary, and subject to this primary holy path.

Spiritual Practice

Examen of Priorities

The Custos' life consists of several chief categories: his relationship with God, his relationship with his wife, his relationship with his children, and then his occupation, friendships, hobbies, and personal endeavors.

Prior to retiring for the evening, first — in a private setting — place yourself in the presence of God the Father. Second, ask Him to help you to identify honestly your current order of priorities. Third, if your priorities are disordered (for example, if work is your top priority and God is third from last in importance), determine what obstacles are to be removed to reestablish proper order. Last, make one small resolution toward reestablishing proper order.

Rule 2

The Analogous Nature of the Custos' Vocation

Let the Custos understand and interpret his relationships, daily responsibilities, obligations, services, trials — in a word, all that constitutes his vocational role and responsibility — as the *analogy of the bridegroom* and the *analogy of fatherhood.*

As a theatrical drama or a novel often expresses an analogy in order to cement a proposed theory or concept in a person's mind in a memorable way, so God uses a man's vocation as husband and father to communicate essential divine truths that draw him more deeply into the mysteries of God's Fatherhood and the mystical marriage of Christ and His Church.

The word *vocation* is drawn from the Latin word *vocare*, "to call," and is related to the word *vox*, meaning "voice." Through the vocation of being a husband and father, the Custos becomes capable of discerning the voice, the Word of God, especially regarding God's fatherhood and Christ's marriage to His Church. Let the Custos understand that God speaks through analogies and that, by comparing his human fatherhood to God's Fatherhood, and his role as a husband to that of Christ the Bridegroom, he will derive great insight regarding God's love and how to love as God.

God always, by means of this analogy, sustains, nourishes, encourages, and blesses the Custos in his vocation, instilling in him an unwavering trust in God, essential wisdom, certain hope of Heaven, and an ever-flowing charity toward God and his neighbor.

Spiritual Practice

Examen of Your Behavior

A child's perception of God the Father often reflects how he perceives his own father, and vice versa.

Prior to retiring for the evening, first — in a private setting — place yourself in the presence of God the Father; second, reflect on the day's conversations, situations, and events involving you, your wife, and your children; third, reflect on how you behaved toward them; fourth, ask yourself: "Would I want God the Father to treat me the way I treat them?" If the answer is "no," visualize how you ought to behave toward your family and begin actualizing that behavior.

Rule 3

The Evil Spirits' Determination to Drive the Custos from His Vocational Path

By means of the analogy of fatherhood and the analogy of the bridegroom, God always encourages man to remain in his calling, as the holy apostle commands: "Every one should remain in the state in which he was called" (1 Cor. 7:20); so also, in a contrary manner, the evil spirits attempt to distract the Custos from and numb him to these vocational analogies for the purpose of robbing him of his courage to remain on this path.

Like a bully who stands in the path of a boy attempting to walk to school, the evil spirits stand in the path of the Custos' vocation to distract and intimidate him, that he might surrender his holy initiative and seek another path. "They set a net for my steps; my soul was bowed down. They dug a pit in my way, but they have fallen into it themselves" (Ps. 57:6).

The intimidations by evil spirits are often cloaked in trials, tests, and tribulations related to the Custos' vocation. Let the Custos be aware that by meditating on these sufferings and finding in them Christ's willingness to suffer for His Church, or God the Father's desire for His children to experience His love and be saved from evil, the very trap set by the evil spirits will become a snare for them; but the Custos will rise from his meditation encouraged. If courage and perseverance are lacking in the Custos, however, it is a certain sign that he is neglecting to reflect upon the *analogy of the bridegroom* and the *analogy of fatherhood* or is resisting the divine counsel contained therein.

Spiritual Practice

Pause and Reflect Prior to Responding

Words have power. Discouraging, demeaning, or disparaging comments are not easily forgotten.

When facing difficulty with your wife or a child, first, recognize your emotions. Are you, for example, tempted to fight or flight? Second, pause before reacting either way (meaning, therefore, that you remain in the presence of the person). Third, in your heart, ask the Holy Spirit for meekness and wisdom. Last, attempt to reassure the other person that you understand by repeating what he or she said and, rather than offering your final statement, ask an honest question that invites conversation.

Usually, the other person will respond more graciously if he or she feels respected and feels that his or her view is attentively listened to and considered.

Rule 4

Signs of Divine Assistance

Let the Custos be aware that God never instills a spirit of pusillanimity or doubt that the Custos can persevere in his noble vocation. On the contrary, the Spirit of God always grants hope, which affords patience, which gives birth to perseverance, which perfects the man in his calling. For as the holy apostle of Christ says, "Count it all joy, my brethren, when you meet various trials, for you know that the testing of your faith produces steadfastness. And let steadfastness have its full effect, that you may be perfect and complete, lacking in nothing" (James 1:2–4). Therefore, where patience, perseverance, and the courage to remain in the calling of Christ are present, there God's will is being accomplished, and the Spirit of Christ is present.

Spiritual Practice

Prayer for Fortitude

When you encounter a minor or severe trial or a test; first, refrain from reacting. Second, choose to respond by asking God for strength, perseverance, and the wisdom to do the very next step. Third, consider St. Teresa of Ávila's prayer of hope:

Let nothing disturb you,
Let nothing frighten you,
All things are passing away.
God never changes.
Patience obtains all things.
Whoever has God lacks nothing.
God alone suffices.

Rule 5

Signs of Demonic Opposition

As God's Spirit is evident in patience, perseverance, hope, and courage, in a contrary manner, the evil spirits instill doubt and discouragement, attempting to convince the Custos that the trials, tests, tribulations, and sufferings he faces are evidence that his vocation is not of God or never was an authentic calling from God, or that God wills him not to remain in his calling, or that his sanctification is impossible by means of his vocation. If the Custos surrenders to any of these lies, he will take steps toward abandoning his post. The evil spirits know that doubt, when consented to, will lead the man to be discouraged. Once lodged in the soul, discouragement leads to disobedience to God's will, and disobedience often results in despairing of God's mercy. Let the Custos be aware that the evil spirits are bent on deceiving him with the lie that the absence of trials is proof of perfection; the truth is that perfection is a result of perseverance through trials. Nevertheless, as the holy apostle says, "For the word of the cross is folly to those who are perishing, but to us who are being saved it is the power of God" (1 Cor. 1:18).

Spiritual Practice

Responding to Disturbing Thoughts

When you are assailed by disturbing or unsettling thoughts, first, identify the doubt. Second, determine whether that doubt tempts you to distrust God the Father's benevolence. If the doubt is causing you to distrust God and His goodness, then, in the name of Jesus Christ, renounce the lie that the doubt is instilling; and lastly, ask the Holy Spirit to give you the opposing virtue. For example, when you are tempted to believe that God has destined you for wrath, claim in the name of Jesus Christ the virtue of the hope of Heaven. When tempted to believe that God is a miser, claim in the name of Jesus Christ the virtue of faith in His generosity. By doing this consistently, the evil spirits will grow weary of being the means for your turning toward God and will depart from you.

Section 3

Counsels Pertaining to the Custos' Authority

Rule 1

The Custos' Office of Headship and Spiritual Authority

As God disclosed to Adam the divine mandates concerning his care for the garden and for his wife, prior to Eve's existence, implying that God had endowed Adam with the responsibility to communicate and transmit those divine mandates to Eve; and as the divine directives given by the angel of God to the Holy Family were disclosed to St. Joseph; so, in the same way, God confirms the man in his vocation as husband and father as having spiritual headship and authority over his family, the domestic church.

This authority is confirmed by God, who approached not the woman who sinned first (Eve) but the man, who received the commands first (Adam). After man's fall from original justice, God did not ask the woman, but only the man, "Where are you?," thus indicating that Adam had fallen from his position of spiritual headship (Gen. 3:11). As God appointed His Son Jesus Christ as head of the Bride, His Church, so also the husband, as an image of Christ, is appointed by God as spiritual head of his wife and his domestic church.

Spiritual Practice

Daily Litany of St. Joseph

Ask St. Joseph to obtain for you the graces to become what he became: *head of a holy family*. Invoke his intercession by means of the recitation of the Litany of St. Joseph (see appendix 1).

Rule 2

Demonic Attack Against the Custos' Office of Headship and Spiritual Authority

Let the Custos be aware that the evil spirits, through the mediums of the world, and at times his wife, and at times those representing the Church, in the name of religion, politics, and equality, will assault and malign the Custos' divinely appointed office of spiritual headship. The evil spirits will attempt to shame the Custos for believing in and exercising his authority by accusing him of being misogynistic or chauvinistic or for believing that he has greater dignity, rights, and privileges than the woman. Argumentation and propaganda, such as the rejection of the equality of rights of women, the dehumanizing and enslaving of women, the domineering and tyrannical abuses of women by men throughout history are some of the accusations that the evil spirits will lodge against the Custos for the purpose of intimidating him and shaming him, in order that he will apologize for his headship and relinquish his vocational role and responsibility.

A ship without a captain will be in disarray. A business cannot function properly without a supervisor, and an army cannot be organized without a leader. Likewise, if the Custos submits to the evil spirits' intimidation and relinquishes his divinely appointed headship, the ship of his family may not reach the shores of Heaven; his family may not prove victorious in the battle against evil and vice. Indeed, the project of the domestic church will be greatly compromised in such a situation, if not fail altogether. For if there is none to lead, none will follow. If a man does not lead his family toward Christ, his family will be led by the evil one away from Christ. The word *devil* comes from the Greek word *diabalos*, a derivative of *diabállein*, which can be translated "to divide." The Custos' headship affords unity in the family, whereas the absence of his authority creates chaos and division.

✝

Spiritual Practice

St. Joseph Invocation to Be Led That You May Lead

Ask St. Joseph to be your mentor and patron, to teach you how to lead your family as he led his. You may do this by means of developing your own personal prayer that asks him to be your leader, spiritual father, and guide. For example:

> *St. Joseph, most gentle and generous, help me to become like you, a father on earth like the Father in heaven. Amen.*
>
> *St. Joseph, lead this ass of a man who carries Jesus and Mary through this land of exile to wherever the Heavenly Father wishes. Amen.*
>
> *St. Joseph, my friend, mentor, spiritual father, and guide, as you protected, provided, and prayed for your family, help me to be a holy protector, provider, and priest of my domestic church. Amen.*

Rule 3

The Custos' Three Modes of Dominion

In the book of Genesis, God granted Adam dominion (Hebrew: *radah*, "to prevail against") over the garden; commanded him to till (Hebrew: *abad*, "to cherish") and keep (Hebrew: *shamar*, "to protect") it; and expected him to transmit the divine commands — particularly, not to partake of the tree of the knowledge of good and evil (obedience to God and His determination of good). Here, God reveals the three modes by which the Custos expresses his dominion for the purpose of prevailing over evil and honoring God: as protector of his family (standing against evil), as provider for his family (working to furnish them with the good things of God), and as priest of his family (transmitting the commands and teachings of God). The Custos exercises his dominion over his domestic church in these three modes so that his family might reveal and reflect the eternal exchange of love between the Divine Persons in the Trinity, which is unity in distinction.

As God in Himself is eternal self-giving love, so also the Custos' dominion is embodied in his gift of self in these three modes (protector, provider, priest) for the purpose of inspiring his family to reflect and relive this divine self-giving love that fosters unity. In giving of himself in this way, he prevails against the kingdom of evil.

Spiritual Practice

Evening Examen of Enemies

Privately, while in the presence of God the Father, first identify the enemies — both temporal and spiritual — that your children and wife need to be protected from. Second, identify and focus on one obstacle or enemy that needs to be removed from your family life. Third, discuss with your wife measures that can be taken to remove that obstacle. Work with your wife to ensure that the obstacle is either partially or entirely removed.

For example, if your children are using mobile devices constantly, you and your wife may determine measures that significantly restrict the use of the devices during family time. Or perhaps your children are watching movies that contain inappropriate content. You and your wife are to determine ways to filter the videos and movies your children watch.

Rule 4

Signs of Divine or Demonic Influence

Let the Custos be aware that the evil spirits have an infernal hatred for the eternal, self-giving, loving relationship of the one, triune God. Therefore, the evil spirits wage a relentless, ongoing war against the human representation of the Trinity — the family — for the purpose of attacking the heart of God. For it is said, "Through the devil's envy death entered the world" (Wisd. 2:24). The evil spirits act as an army, laying siege against the fortified kingdom that is the domestic church, intent on dethroning, sidelining, or imprisoning its king (the father) for the purpose of plundering his goods (his wife and children) (see Mark 3:27). Know that the triune God is selfless and united and that the devil and his kingdom are selfish and divided. Therefore, when the father is inspired toward self-giving love, the Spirit of Almighty God is present; and when the father acts in a selfish manner, the devil is influencing the Custos. The more the Custos acts in selflessness, the more his family will be united in Christ; whereas the more the Custos acts in selfishness, the more his family will be divided.

Spiritual Practice

Identify One Act of Selfless Service

Every family has multiple responsibilities, duties, and chores that assist in the ordering of family life. Identify one duty, chore, or responsibility that your wife or children do and intentionally assist in that duty to lighten their burden.

For example, if the children are cleaning the kitchen after dinner, rather than relaxing or doing something for yourself, assist them and so lighten their load. Make the most of this time by conversing and engaging with them.

Rule 5

The Custos' Post Between the Family and the World

In the beginning, God created Adam outside the garden (see Gen. 2), a symbol of the unsubdued world, and later placed the man in the garden, a symbol of the domestic life and its fruitfulness. This indicates that Adam's twofold purpose is to subdue the world by cultivating, hunting, and gathering its fruits for his family, while also protecting his family from the pernicious influences of the world.

In a similar way, the Custos is appointed by God to subdue the world, reaping its good fruits for his family, while also protecting his family from being subdued by the world, the flesh, and the devil. He is to have dominion over the world and not let the world have dominion over his estate. As a shepherd lies down at the sheepgate to protect his sheep from wolves, the husband and father stands at his post, always aware that there is an enemy at large from whom he is to protect the flock of his family — if necessary, by laying down his life.

Spiritual Practice

Evening Examen of One's Guardianship

God gave Adam the duty to protect Eve and the garden, yet he failed to protect not only them but also himself. Protecting others from evil begins with protecting oneself from malicious forces.

During your evening examen, reflect on how you have allowed the serpent — that is, the devil — to slither past your wall of defense. Then ask God the Father for the strength and the resolve to repent of this vice.

In order for a vice to be removed effectively, it must be replaced with something virtuous. Therefore, identify also one thing that you will do to replace with a virtue the vice to which you are attached.

Rule 6

Signs That the Evil Spirits Are Conditioning the Custos to Be a Hireling

Let the Custos be aware that, though he is a shepherd who stands post at the threshold between the world and his family, the evil spirits will make every attempt to entice him with prestige, prominence, accolades, honors, the addiction of work, human respect, a life of comfort, disordered sensuality, and love of riches. If he succumbs to any of these distractions in a habitual manner—without repenting—he will become a hireling who, upon encountering hardship in his marriage and family, in financial difficulties, or in the realization of the lack of worldly success in all of its forms, will flee from his post by being negligent in his vocational duties, by being apathetic toward his family, by being spiritually slothful in his response to God, or by leaving his post as guardian of his family altogether. If any of these characteristics are increasing in the Custos, let him be aware that the evil one is at hand, bent on the ruin of his domestic church.

Spiritual Practice

Protect Your Family from Your Work

Consistently return home from work on time. Silence the phone during family time. Guard your conversations from work topics.

Rule 7

The Custos' Warrior Spirit

Let the Custos understand that if he is to overcome and vanquish diabolical enemies, it is necessary that he ask the Holy Spirit to give him God's warrior spirit. As it is written, "The Lord is a man of war; the Lord is His name" (Exod. 15:3). The warrior spirit is embodied by a man who knows that he is at war with evil for the "glorious liberty of the children of God" (Rom. 8:21).

In his determination to be victorious in the spiritual battle, the Custos takes up the spiritual arms of daily prayer, fasting, mortification, meditations, and examens, all of which together constitute the shield of faith — that is, an unwavering trust in God the Father. For, as it is written, "without faith it is impossible to please [God]" (Heb 11:6). Added to these is the divine sustenance of the sacraments, particularly the Most Holy Eucharist and Reconciliation. Using these weapons, the Custos will become skilled at spiritual warfare and be consistently victorious over evil.

Spiritual Practice

Attend One Additional Holy Mass per Week

Identify a weekday morning on which you can consistently attend Holy Mass. Commit yourself to attending Mass on that day each week.

Rule 8

Signs That the Evil Spirits Are Conquering the Warrior Spirit

Let the Custos be aware that withdrawal from private prayer or the sacraments, resistance to confessing his sins sacramentally, lack of trust in God the Father, tepidity toward corporal mortifications or acts of service, or an unwillingness to examine his conscience are certain signs that the evil spirits are gaining influence over him.

Spiritual Practice

Biweekly Confession

Find out your parish's times for the Sacrament of Reconciliation. Commit yourself to going to Confession biweekly.

Rule 9

The Custos' Spirit of the Beloved

Though the Custos is to have God's warrior spirit, he can become hardened, fatigued, and desensitized from the hardships and sufferings caused by the spiritual battle. Accompanying signs of demonic weariness are a loss of joy and impatience with and contempt for others — especially those of his own family — rather than compassion for them. Additionally, the Custos begins to perceive the divine commands as a burden, or he embraces them militaristically and his spirituality bears the mark of legalism, repression, and the condemnation of others. If his relationship with God is exclusively as that of a soldier to his general, he will eventually lack charity, and his attitude toward God will be like that of a mercenary.

To balance the warrior spirit, the Custos is to ask the Holy Spirit for the spirit of a lover. The spirit of the lover tempers the man of battle with compassion, tenderness, understanding, counsel, and above all, charity. For as the holy apostle says, among all gifts, "the greatest of these is love" (1 Cor. 13:13).

To love his bride as Christ the Bridegroom loves His Church, the Custos must become one who is loved by the Bridegroom. That is, he must allow himself to receive such love. This places the man in a challenging position. By his own means, he is incapable of loving his wife in the manner in which Christ loves His Church; therefore, it is imperative that he humble himself as a "bride" of Christ, or a "beloved soul" of Christ, and by being loved as the beloved, he will learn how to love his beloved — his wife — as Christ loves him.

Spiritual Practice

Bridegroom Prayer

The warrior lover often needs to learn to be loved. To become receptive to the Divine Bridegroom's affection and charity, pray often:

> *Come, Lord Jesus, come. The Spirit and the Bride say, "Come" (see Rev. 22:17).*

Section 4

Counsels Pertaining to the Custos' Marriage

Rule 1

The Custos' Marriage Is Analogous to Christ's Relationship with His Church

As Christ is Bridegroom to His Church, so also the Custos is husband to his wife. As Christ is lover to the Church, His beloved, so also the Custos intentionally initiates acts of love toward his wife. The Custos' marriage, by extension of the analogy, is to become an efficacious sign of Christ's *fidelity* to and *charity* for His Church. For the holy apostle, speaking of the marriage bond, says, "This is a great sacrament; but I speak of Christ and of the Church" (Eph. 5:32). Let the Custos understand that a great portion of his mission is to transmit God's love and fidelity by means of his marriage. His marriage has the purpose of reflecting "the light to the nations" (see Lk 2:32; Isa. 49:6) while also reflecting his fidelity: "For I hate divorce, says the Lord the God of Israel" (Mal. 2:16). If his actions toward his wife are marked by fidelity and charity, the Custos is becoming a sacrament of Christ; if his disposition toward his wife is one of contempt, resent, utility, neglect, or indifference, he is failing to reflect Christ and is allowing himself to be used as a tool of the devil. Therefore, let the Custos look to the life of Christ and study how He related to sinners and then commit himself to reflecting His love, fidelity, and forgiveness — particularly to his wife.

Spiritual Practice

Pray for Your Wife Daily

As part of your daily morning prayer, pray for God's blessing upon your wife. Pray that you may love her as Christ, the Divine Bridegroom, loves and sacrifices Himself for His Bride, the Church.

Rule 2

The Exaltation of the Custos' Wife as Queen of His Domestic Church

Let the Custos understand that he is to honor his wife as his queen, striving always to become more aware of her interior beauty, her dignity, and her holiness and to foster her progress toward union with God. St. Thomas Aquinas quotes this axiom of the philosopher Aristotle: "What is first in the order of intention is last in the order of execution";[3] and he applies it to Eve, who comes last in the created order, which indicates that woman is the pinnacle of God's intention. All of creation is ordered toward woman's life-bearing gift. Mary, both Queen of Heaven and earth and the Mother of the Son of God, is rightly hailed as the New Eve, the fulfillment of Eve. Therefore, as the fulfillment of Eve, she is truly primary in God's intention as the God-bearer (*Theotokos*), and all of creation is ordered toward her and the fruit of her womb, Jesus.

As Christ shares the authority and power of His kingship with Mary, His Queen, because of her motherhood and because of her union with Him in His Passion and death (bride in suffering), so let the husband also share his power and authority with his wife. The greater the honor rendered to Mary the Queen, the greater the honor rendered to Christ the King. As Christ glorifies the Church, His Bride, so is He glorified in His Church. Therefore, if a husband exalts his wife, so also will he be exalted.

[3] *Summa Theologiae*, I-II, q. 25.

Spiritual Practice

Ask God to See Your Wife's Beauty Anew

Often, as the years pass, a husband can begin to fail to perceive his wife's emotional, intellectual, spiritual, and physical beauty. Therefore, pray daily that Our Lord Jesus, the Divine Bridegroom, will allow you the vision to perceive anew your wife's beauty.

Rule 3

Two Primary Temptations Against the Custos' Queen

Regarding the honor and respect due to his queen, let the Custos be aware that the evil spirits will tempt him in one of two primary ways: abdication or domination. On one hand, the evil spirits will condition the Custos to exalt his wife in such a highly disordered way that he relinquishes or surrenders much of his divinely instituted office of headship. If he abdicates his office and authority, the fruitfulness of his vocational role and responsibility will be hindered greatly, or abolished altogether, rendering him spiritually neutered.

On the other hand, the evil spirits will attempt to convince the man that his wife and her role are less important in rank, dignity, position, and honor than his own. If he believes this demonic lie—even subconsciously—he will inevitably dominate her, objectify her, demean her, disrespect her, and treat her as a servant rather than as his equal partner. Let the Custos be aware that both dispositions are gravely disordered. This indebtedness is expressed most perfectly by the Custos' fidelity to his wife by serving her and reverencing her for love of Christ.

Spiritual Practice

One Act of Hidden Service for Your Wife

First, identify an area of need that your wife has. For example, it could be a small project that she has been wanting to complete or something that needs to be moved from one part of the house to another. Second, without telling her and without grumbling, complete the act of service for her. Lastly, do not seek recognition for it. Simply offer the act of love to God for her salvation and sanctification.

Rule 4

The Means Through Which the Custos Receives His Vocation

As a man receives his surname from his father and that name expresses the unbroken lineage of his ancestral heritage, in a similar way, the Custos receives his fatherly vocation from God primarily and through his wife secondarily. Therefore, the Custos is indebted not only to God but also to his wife; thus, let him thank both for his noble calling. For as St. Joseph received his noble mission of being a father to the Son of God through Mary, his wife, and therefore is eternally indebted to her, so also a husband receives his noble mission by means of his wife and therefore is indebted to her.

Spiritual Practice

One Daily Act of Affirmation or Encouragement for Your Wife

First, reflect on the many and varied ways in which your wife is a gift to you. Second, identify one of those characteristics. Third, and by text, e-mail, or phone or in person, affirm your wife and encourage her by telling her how much you admire that quality that she possesses. For example: "Honey, I thank God for your joy. You bring me so much happiness."

Rule 5

Two Methods the Evil Spirits Use Against the Custos' Indebtedness to His Wife

Regarding the fact that the Custos receives his fatherhood and office of charitable authority (Greek: *oikodespotes*) through his wife and therefore is indebted to her, let the Custos be aware that the evil spirits will tempt him regarding this truth in two primary ways. First, they will tempt him to believe that he is so indebted to his wife for the gift of his vocation that he must relinquish his charitable authority to her. Let the Custos be aware that although St. Joseph is indebted to the Blessed Virgin Mary, who is full of grace and is the fairest and most pure and resplendent of all creatures, God nevertheless confirmed Joseph's spiritual authority as Custos and Head of the Holy Family (all divine directives regarding the Holy Family were transmitted through the angel of God to Joseph) — a divinely appointed authority that he did not mitigate, relinquish, or diminish.

Second, the evil spirits will tempt the Custos to resent or reject his wife and her motherhood — that is, the very means by which he has received his call. It is possible that a man, after encountering the demands of the role and responsibility of the Custos, subconsciously or even consciously lays blame upon his wife for his situation and desires to be free of her. Though St. Joseph encountered many hardships because of the Blessed Virgin Mary's God-given mission, he did not become embittered or resentful toward her; rather, he used his authority to exalt and honor her.

Spiritual Practice

Thank God for Your Wife

During your morning prayer or evening examen, simply praise God for creating your wife and for giving her to you as your wife. Thank Him often for this gift.

Rule 6

The Temptation to Flee from One's Wife

If the Custos divorces himself from his wife, he severs his relationship with his wife primarily, but also, secondarily, he separates himself from, if not lays siege to, his fatherly vocation — his call from God. As the holy apostle says, "Every one should remain in the state in which he was called" (1 Cor. 7:20). And again, "So, brethren, in whatever state each was called, there let him remain with God" (1 Cor. 7:24). Therefore, let the Custos, when faced with the temptation to flee from his wife, look to the faithful example of Christ, who loves His Bride, especially when she is indifferent or unfaithful to Him; by following that example, he will surely abide with God by means of his fidelity to his wife.

Spiritual Practice

One Hidden Sacrifice for Your Wife

We sacrifice for that which we love. If we lack love, we should increase our sacrifice so that our love may increase. Each day, identify one small hidden sacrifice you can make on behalf of your wife; for example: skipping a meal, taking a cold shower, sleeping on the floor, or drinking only water. Offer it to God secretly so that His love may fill your wife more and that your love for her may increase.

Rule 7

The Manner in Which the Custos Is to Embrace His Wife

A husband is to embrace his wife in the manner that St. Paul outlines in the fifth chapter of his Letter to the Ephesians. Thrice the holy apostle exhorts the husband to "love." At the beginning of the passage: "Husbands, love your wives, as Christ loved the Church and gave himself up for her" (Eph. 5:25); in the middle of the passage: "Even so husbands should love their wives as their own bodies. He who loves his wife loves himself" (Eph. 5:28); and at the end of the passage: "Let each one of you love his wife as himself, and let the wife see that she respects her husband" (Eph. 5:33).

The word rendered "love" is the Greek word *agape*, which can be defined as a selfless, disinterested, pure, unconditional, sacrificial love — the love that God has for His children and the love that Christ has for His Church. Agape is the highest form of charity, and it transcends and endures all circumstances.

Let the Custos be aware that to fulfill the command to love one's wife is the highest form of charity, for it is to "love one another as I have loved you" (John 15:12). Additionally, God created Eve to be Adam's *helpmate* (Hebrew: *ezer chenegdo*), which can be translated as an "essential counterpart," or another self, as the right hand is to the left.

Therefore, a husband is to reflect upon the attention and care that he gives to his own desires, initiatives, and sufferings and then compare those to the attention and care that he gives to his wife. By doing so, he can determine whether he is fulfilling this great command to love her in the way that he loves himself and thus fulfill the second part of the greatest commandment.

✝

Spiritual Practice

Evening Examen on Prioritizing Your Wife

During your evening examen, first, place yourself in the presence of God the Father. Second, reflect on those aspects of your life that most demand your attention or that you find most desirable. Then ask God to help you see whether you have given the same attention to your wife's desires and aspirations as to yours. If not, identify one of your wife's desires and make it your own. Work at helping her to achieve that endeavor as though it were your own.

Rule 8

The Custos' Incapacity to Fulfill the Law of Love Without Christ

Let the Custos be aware that, of his own power and will, he is incapable of loving his wife as Christ loves the Church. As Our Lord said, "Apart from me you can do nothing" (John 15:5). Therefore, it is imperative that in his weakness, the Custos depend upon Christ entirely. For as the holy apostle says, "I can do all things in him who strengthens me" (Phil 4:13); and "with God nothing will be impossible" (Luke 1:37). A saying sometimes attributed to the holy Doctor St. Augustine is "One cannot give what one does not possess." Therefore, let the Custos make every effort first to abide in Christ, so that Christ may abide in him and that he may thus give Christ's love to his wife.

As the Custos' love for God increases, so will his ability to love his wife increase. If his love for God becomes indifferent or hostile, so eventually will his love for his wife become indifferent or hostile. Therefore, let the Custos examine how he loves his wife; this will be a good indication of how he loves God.

Spiritual Practice

EVENING EXAMEN ON LOVE FOR YOUR WIFE

During your evening examen, first, place yourself in the presence of God the Father. Second, reflect on the following three categories as they pertain to your wife: communication, attention, and affirmation. In each of these three categories, rate yourself as honestly as you can, from 1 (least) to 5 (best). Select an area that needs improvement, and commit to one small act of love that could improve that area. Pray often:

Lord Jesus, help me to love her as You love her.

Rule 9

The Need for the Custos to Love Himself So That He May Also Love His Wife

Let the Custos understand that he is to love his wife as Christ loves her (see John 15:13). Therefore, God wills always that a man receives and trusts in His fatherly love and, by doing so, that he learns to love himself as God loves him. The evil spirits, on the contrary, are always bent on disrupting and undermining the Custos' trust in God the Father. Without trusting that God the Father loves the man as His own son, the man will eventually lack love for himself; as his love for himself is diminished, or absent, he will become less capable of loving his wife. She will begin to starve emotionally and spiritually and, eventually — if left unchecked — she will interiorly resent her husband, believing him to be pusillanimous, which could plant within her heart the seed of infidelity.

Let the Custos know that, to the degree that he loves himself as God loves him, to that same extent he will be capable of loving his wife.

✛

Spiritual Practice

Establish Your Prayer Place

Carve out a small area in your home, away from everything else — particularly those things that are most distracting. Sanctify it with religious objects: a Bible, a prayer chair, perhaps a kneeler, an altar, and so forth. Commit yourself to meeting with God in this prayer place daily. During your prayer, try not to address God as "God" or "Lord" but as "Abba, Father." When you do this, you will not only demonstrate that the Holy Spirit lives in you (see Gal. 4:6), but also your relationship with God will become more trusting and tender.

Rule 10

The Three Sacred Duties of a Husband

According to the holy apostle, the Custos has three primary spiritual duties in relation to his wife. First, he is to deliver himself up for his wife, for the sacred text reads, "Husbands, love your wives, as Christ loved the Church and gave himself up for her" (Eph 5:25). Second, the Custos is to assist in his wife's sanctification, for the Scripture says, "Christ loved the church and gave himself up for her, that he might sanctify her, having cleansed her by the washing of water with the word" (Eph. 5:25–26). Third, the Custos is to present his wife to God, as Christ presents "the church to himself in splendor, without spot or wrinkle or any such thing, that she might be holy and without blemish" (Eph. 5:27).

Spiritual Practice

Prayer with Your Wife

Each evening, spend several minutes in prayer with your wife. First, discuss beforehand what petitions the two of you have; second, pray together, voicing those petitions; and last, end your prayer time by thanking God the Father for your marriage and ask His blessing to be upon it.

Rule 11

The Custos' Sacred Duty to Deliver Himself Up for His Wife

Let the Custos understand that he is to deliver himself up for his wife, as Christ delivered Himself up for the Church. The Greek word for "deliver," *paradōken*, means "to hand over," "to give," or "to deliver over." This is the same word that Our Lord uses to describe God the Father's generosity: "If you then, who are evil, know how to give good gifts to your children, how much more will your Father who is in heaven give [*paradōken*] good things to those who ask him!" (Matt. 7:11). Furthermore, this generosity is not limited to giving things only; it also includes the sharing of one's authority, as Christ shared His authority with His disciples: "And he called to him his twelve disciples and gave [*paradōken*] them authority over unclean spirits, to cast them out, and to heal every disease and every infirmity" (Matt. 10:1). Therefore, let the husband deliver himself up to God on behalf of his wife by generously sharing and entrusting to God his talents, gifts, goods, love, authority, and power, with his wife as his equal, his essential counterpart.

Spiritual Practice

Weekly Date Night

If your wife is to believe that she is most important in your life, your actions must reflect that reality. A husband demonstrates that his wife is his top priority (save God) by having a scheduled weekly date night. If a weekly date night is impossible due to the needs of small children or the lack of babysitting options, aim for every other week or at least once a month.

First, establish the day and time for your date night. Second, keep it simple. It does not need to be expensive or extravagant. Third, silence all mobile devices or leave them in the car. Fourth, whether you are having a disagreement or the conversation is going well, rest in that time without cutting it short. During your date, reassure your wife that you love her, that you admire her beauty, and by listening attentively, that you respect her.

Rule 12

Two Demonic Tactics Against the Custos' Headship

Let the Custos be aware that the evil spirits will make every attempt to convince him to maintain the upper hand in regard to power and authority, convincing him to be restrictive with his gift of self. The holy pontiff St. John Paul II exhorts the husband to ensure that his wife does not "become a servant or slave of the husband and an object of unilateral domination."[4]

On the other hand, the evil spirits will shame the Custos for exercising his kingly authority by convincing him that "being subject to one another out of reverence for Christ" (see Eph. 5:21) releases him from his office of authority.

Let the Custos be aware that mutual subjection among spouses cannot occur without a cause or an initiating force. Thus, mutual submission and a sharing of authority presupposes that the authority originates in and proceeds from the husband. As our Lord says, "The kings of the Gentiles exercise lordship over them; and those in authority over them are called benefactors. But not so with you; rather let the greatest among you become as the youngest, and the leader as one who serves" (Luke 22:25–26). Therefore, to lead with authority is to serve, and to serve with authority presupposes that the husband has been granted such authority from God. To use one's authority to dominate, or to dismiss one's authority for fear of dominating, is not of God.

[4] John Paul II, *Theology of the Body: Human Love in the Divine Plan* (Boston: Pauline Books and Media, 1997), 310.

Spiritual Practice

Ten Minutes of Daily Intentional Time with Your Wife

Toward the end of the day, pause, try to relax, and sit down with your wife for ten minutes or more. The purpose of this is, first, to hear her heart and discern how she is feeling — physically, emotionally, and psychologically — and, second, by sitting with her, without distractions, to reassure her that you desire her. Try to refrain from "fixing" her problems; rather, affirm her.

Rule 13

The Custos' Sacred Duty to Foster His Wife's Sanctification

Let the husband understand that he is responsible for fostering his wife's sanctification, for Scripture says, "Christ loved the church and gave himself up for her, that he might *sanctify* her, having cleansed her by the washing of water with the word" (Eph. 5:25–26, emphasis added). The Custos is responsible for fostering and encouraging his wife in the ways of God, that she may be *sacred* (Greek: *hagios*) — holy and set apart for God. He is to accomplish this in three ways. First, he does this by protecting her from being assimilated by the world, for, as the holy apostle says, "whoever wishes to be a friend of the world makes himself an enemy of God" (James 4:4). Second, the Custos is to protect his wife from his own disordered desires, particularly by seeing her as an object of lust or by reducing her to being his servant. Lust separates love from sacrifice, and sacrifice (particularly of himself and his disordered desires) is the duty of the priest of the domestic church. As the holy apostle says, "Present your bodies as a living sacrifice, holy and acceptable to God" (Rom. 12:1). Third, the Custos is to protect his wife from the evil one by guarding her relationship with God — primarily by embodying the love of God and being a living reflection of God the Father and Christ the Divine Bridegroom; and secondarily, by ensuring that she has adequate time for prayer and meditation, so that she may be renewed and strengthened for the tasks of her vocation.

Spiritual Practice

Protect Your Wife's Prayer Time

First, do not force or coerce your wife into praying. Invite her. This has already been established by your praying your petitions together with your wife. In addition to "couple prayer," she may desire to pray privately. First, ask her if she needs time and space to pray. Second, ask her what you can do to help her in this endeavor. Third, follow through.

For example: If she needs prayer time after dinner, offer to clean the kitchen with the children. If that has been finished, play a game with the children, take them outside, or something similar. If your wife needs a special place to pray, help create that for her.

Rule 14

The Custos' Sacred Duty to Bless His Wife

Let the Custos understand that God has granted him the authority to bless his wife in the name of Jesus Christ and the Most Holy Trinity. By means of this blessing, God forges a deep bond between spouses that is most difficult for the evil spirits to disrupt or overcome. In the moment of the blessing, the Custos images the sweetness, tenderness, sacrificial love, and courage of the Divine Bridegroom Jesus Christ. Therefore, let the Custos bless his wife daily, imploring God to bless her, to favor her with His grace, to protect her from all evil, and to grant her eternal communion with the Most Holy Trinity.

Spiritual Practice

Bless Your Wife Daily

First, identify a consistent time to bless your wife (typically, prior to bedtime is best). Second, trace the Sign of the Cross on her forehead. Third, invoke God's blessing upon her. While tracing the Sign of the Cross on her forehead, pray the following:

> *May the Lord bless you and keep you. May His face shine kindly upon you. May the Lord grant you His kindness and peace all your days, that you may behold His face in the marriage that never ends. Abba, Father, protect my wife from all evil and bring her safely into Your eternal embrace. Amen.*

Rule 15

The Evil Spirits' Intention to Deter the Custos from Blessing His Wife

Let the Custos be aware that as God wills him to bless his wife, the evil spirits, on the contrary, will make every attempt to deter him from blessing her. The evil spirits will attempt to instill fear, embarrassment, or a sense of unworthiness in the mind of the Custos. Additionally, the evil spirits will make every attempt to imprison him in a state of mortal sin so that he may not transmit grace to his wife. Let the Custos take courage in knowing that these are signs that the evil spirits have a great hatred for the power derived from his act of blessing his wife. Let him make every effort to remain in a state of grace, and if he is not, let him sacramentally confess his sins as soon as he is able, that he may become a channel of grace for his wife.

Spiritual Practice

Confess Your Sins Sacramentally

First, examine your conscience. Second, allow God to convict you of those behaviors and acts that are injustices against Him and His children. Third, "take with you words and return to the Lord" (Hos. 14:2) — that is, thoughtfully determine what you will say and sacramentally confess your sins. And lastly, be certain to thank God for His mercy after completing your confession.

Rule 16

The Evil Spirits' Desire to Remove the Mother's Influence from Her Children

As God wills that the Custos protect his wife from the world, the flesh, and the devil, the evil spirits, on the contrary, will attempt to seduce and convince the wife (and her husband) to conform to the world and its maxims. According to the holy pontiff John Paul II, the preferential and natural place for a woman is in the home, and yet there exist certain conditions that sometimes demand that women work outside the home.[5] Considering this, the evil spirits will use those conditions in order to tempt the woman to believe that she will receive more honor, respect, and fulfillment by working outside the home than by embracing the saintly vocation of motherhood. Additionally, the evil spirits will instill the fear into the married couple that the husband's income will not be capable of providing for the family; or that the family will benefit from a dual income and that therefore both the husband and the wife must work outside the home. By instilling fear, inducing covetousness, and promising to satisfy the desire of greed, which is idolatry (see Eph. 5:5), the evil spirits will attempt to remove the mother's influence from her children, in order that the world may indoctrinate them. This often results in a miserly attitude toward bearing children and an increased temptation to use contraception. This is no small matter. If it be in his power, the Custos is to protect and provide for his wife's vocation of motherhood by

[5] Pope St. John Paul II, apostolic exhortation *Familiaris Consortio* (November 22, 1981), no. 23.

allowing her to remain in her home. Let the Custos always remain hopeful, believing that God will provide.

Spiritual Practice

Discuss Your Wife's Needs Regarding Child-Rearing and Occupation

During your date night or ten-minute evening conversations, ask your wife:

If she works outside the home: *Do you want to work outside the home? What would be ideal for you?*

If she is a stay-at-home wife: *Do you have time for yourself and for friendships? What do you need socially?*

The purpose of having this conversation is to ensure that your personal and parenting goals are aligned.

Rule 17

The Custos' Sacred Duty to Present His Wife to God

Let the Custos be aware that he and his wife and their perpetual pledge of fidelity to one another constitute the Sacrament of Matrimony. They are no longer two, but one flesh. Even though the spouses are distinct persons, they are one in Matrimony. The vow of fidelity in good times and in bad, in sickness and in health, in poverty and in riches, till death separates the spouses, coupled with the two being one flesh, indicates that the Custos is to live according to the maxim that husband and wife "bear one another's burdens, and so fulfil the law of Christ" (Gal. 6:2). Therefore, let the Custos *present* his wife to God "that she might be holy and without blemish" (Eph. 5:27).

To present his wife to God demands that the husband stand firm in his relationship with her, fostering an intimacy with her that ever deepens his knowledge of her. This knowledge of his wife, including her spiritual and corporal burdens and desires, he presents to God in prayer — in union with himself. As mentioned previously, the husband is to understand his wife as a completion of himself; therefore, if he neglects to present his wife and her needs to God, his presentation of himself to God is incomplete.

Spiritual Practice

Don't Assume Your Wife's Needs — Ask Her

Often, we men can assume that we know our wives and what they need. Quite often, however, a wife wants to be asked what she needs.

First, during your date night or evening ten-minute conversations, ask your wife how she is doing emotionally, physically, spiritually, and so forth. Second, ask her if there is anything you can do to help address her needs. Third, creatively and with intentionality, and without complaining or boasting, begin to address her needs. This will help your wife realize: "He truly cares about me."

Rule 18

The Honor That the Custos Owes His Wife

Let the husband, above all, honor his wife. For when Adam, after awakening from the divinely induced supernatural slumber, set his gaze upon his wife, Eve, for the first time, he praised her with honor and jubilation as he spoke these words: "This at last is bone of my bones and flesh of my flesh; she shall be called Woman, because she was taken out of Man" (Gen. 2:23). In other words, "I am in her, and she is in me, and we together are one flesh." Therefore, the husband establishes his relationship with his wife as primary over all relationships, save that of his relationship with God. He demonstrates this primacy by serving her, cherishing her, respecting her, spending time with her individually, and delighting in her, reverencing her with words of affirmation and praise — particularly in the presence of his children — counting her as better than himself. For as the holy apostle says, "Do nothing from selfishness or conceit, but in humility count others [your wife] better than yourselves. Let each of you look not only to his own interests, but also to the interests of others" (Phil 2:3–4), particularly the interests of his wife.

Spiritual Practice

Affirm Your Wife in Front of Your Children

While your children are present, affirm your wife's personality or beauty or your admiration for one of her particular qualities. When you are with your children and your wife is not present, speak highly of her, intentionally admiring her. This speaks volumes to your children, increasing their respect and admiration for her.

Rule 19

How the Evil Spirits Will Tempt the Custos to Have Contempt for His Wife

The evil one hates woman and has an infernal contempt for her ability to give birth to children, who bear the image of God. Though the evil spirits' hatred is for all women, they despise the Most Holy Virgin Mary in particular, for she is the ultimate "Bride of Christ," daughter of God the Father, and spouse of the Holy Spirit. She is the ultimate life-bearer (*Theotokos*), in that she gave birth to Life itself — the Word incarnate.

Let the Custos be aware that the evil spirits will strive to instill contempt in his heart for the Blessed Virgin Mary, for women universally, and particularly for his own wife. In regard to his wife, this contempt will become manifest first in interior judgments; second, in verbal criticisms that demean her physical and emotional character and her performance in her duties; third, in distancing of himself from her emotionally; and fourth, in eventual separation from her.

Therefore, let the Custos examine the manner in which he speaks of and to his wife — as the Lord says, "Out of the abundance of the heart the mouth speaks" (Matt. 12:34) — while also determining whether he is maintaining emotional intimacy with her or is withdrawing from her. This will assist him in assessing his true interior disposition toward her. If he speaks ill of her, or is distancing himself from her, let him repent and seek forgiveness and assistance from God immediately, and God will provide the charity necessary to fulfill his vocation. Yet, if he continues in his fallen and sinful ways, refusing to repent, he will become a tool of the devil and will transmit the sin and wound of misogyny to his children.

Additionally, let the Custos be aware that devotion to the Blessed Virgin Mary will serve as a sure remedy for any lack of love for his wife, for she obtained from her Son the miracle of new wine — a rich symbol of the grace of the Lord Jesus — at a marriage feast (see John 2). Therefore, she can also obtain the grace necessary for the healing of a marriage, if she is invited into the sacrament. As the Custos' devotion to the Blessed Virgin Mary increases, so will his devotion to his wife.

Spiritual Practice

Daily Decade of the Rosary for Your Marriage

Pray the second Luminous Mystery of the Rosary of the Blessed Virgin Mary: Christ transforms the water into wine at His Mother's bidding. While reflecting on this mystery, pray that Our Lady will obtain from her Son the grace that the water of your marriage (your human efforts) will be transformed into wine — that is, the grace-filled healing that unifies your marriage in a living reflection of Christ and His Church.

Rule 20

The Custos' Response to His Wife's Lack of Respect for Him

Let the Custos be aware that the evil spirits will take advantage of the occasions on which he does not receive the desired respect, affirmation, and intimacies from his wife or of the apparent diminishing of his wife's physical beauty with age; with these motivations, the evil spirits will entice and lure him to dishonor his wife or to seek such consolations elsewhere. The evil spirits will use the absence of respect and affirmation from his wife to try to convince the Custos that he is justified in dishonoring his bride or in being unfaithful to her. Yet let the Custos turn toward Christ the Bridegroom and His holy example. It was not Christ's condemnation that inspired the sinner to return to Him but the sacrifice of Himself expressed by His mercy and forgiveness. As the Mystical Doctor said, "Where there is no love, put love, and there will be love."[6] Therefore, if respect from the Custos' wife is lacking, he is all the more to place love in her midst by expressions of mercy, acts of disinterested service, and forgiveness.

[6] St. John of the Cross, Letter 26 to Madre María de la Encarnación in Segovia, July 6, 1591.

Spiritual Practice

Offering Oneself for One's Wife

When you encounter difficulties relating to your wife, such as her aging or changing, or an uneven interest between the two of you in physical intimacy, or the like, offer yourself to God on her behalf, praying, "This is my body, given for you." By uniting your offering of yourself to the offering of Christ, the Father will bless your wife and your marriage. Additionally, He will change the way you see her. Often, for things to change, we need to change the way we see them.

Rule 21

The Essential Nature of Trust in Marriage

Trust is the essential, fundamental foundation of every true and enduring relationship, especially in the Sacrament of Marriage. A husband is to ask God's assistance and apply the grace that he receives for the purpose of forging an ever-increasing bond of trust between him and his wife. For if trust is established, there will be honest vulnerability between the spouses. If vulnerability is present, intimacy between spouses will be deepened. If intimacy is deepened, accountability will become habitual and well received. If accountability is well received, the two will manifest the love of God; and in manifesting the love of God, they will become living saints. Let the Custos be aware that his greatest effort in his marriage is to build the bond of trust by means of countless acts of vulnerability. He accomplishes this by allowing his inner sentiments to be revealed to his wife charitably and by assuring her that she can safely share her inner sentiments with him charitably, without his rejecting or judging her. If the Custos is consistent in his efforts to forge the bond of trust between him and his wife, then, when he does fail her (and he will, for he is a fallen human), she will be more ready to forgive him and to labor for the restoration of the bond of trust between them. As the proverb says, "A righteous man falls seven times, and rises again" (Prov. 24:16). Our Lord says, regarding how many times a man should forgive one who has offended him, "I do not say to you seven times, but seventy times seven" (Matt. 18:22). In other words, the husband will fall many times, but if he lays the foundation of trust in his marriage, he will assist his wife in fulfilling the Lord's command to forgive him. Conversely, if trust is established with his wife, the Custos will become more willing and able to forgive her for her failings.

†

Spiritual Practice

Ask Your Wife for Forgiveness

When you have had an argument or a disagreement with your wife, first focus on your offense or negligence in the matter; second, claim or own your infraction; third, apologize to her.

When apologizing, however, refrain from saying only "I'm sorry," as that is only a statement as to how you feel and allows you to retain control. Rather, always go on to ask, "Will you forgive me?" This is very humbling and meek, and it will give your wife the power to forgive.

Additionally, refrain from saying, "I was wrong, but *you* did ..." When apologizing and asking for forgiveness, never point out your wife's wrong, as that cheapens and undermines what ought to be an unstinting and unqualified action on your part. Allow her to claim her shortcomings herself rather than accusing her of them.

All of this wins her over to love.

Rule 22

The Temptation Toward Infidelity

Let the Custos be aware that the evil spirits will condition, lure, entice, and tempt him to break the bond of fidelity between him and his wife; they know that holy marriages are the foundation of holy families, that holy families are the foundation of a Holy Church, and that it is a Holy Church that brings about the conversion of sinners. The evil spirits know that if the Custos is ensnared in ongoing, habitual sin, the Kingdom of God will be hindered.

As the holy apostle says, "Each person is tempted when he is lured and enticed by his own desire. Then desire when it has conceived gives birth to sin; and sin when it is full-grown brings forth death" (James 1:14–15). And as the proverb says, "He who conceals his transgressions will not prosper, but he who confesses and forsakes them will obtain mercy" (Prov. 28:13).

The evil spirits will lure a man into sin, and then, after he has sinned, they will plague him to conceal that sin in darkness. Yet the more his sin remains in darkness, the more power it has over him. The power of the sin, especially sexual infidelity, leads a man to the addiction or habituation of that disordered and evil action. When this occurs, the Custos' ability to be a "good steward of God's varied grace" (see 1 Pet. 4:10) has been severed, and he and his marriage will certainly not prosper. The evil spirits will especially tempt the Custos to commit sexual, emotional, and financial infidelity while also conditioning him to develop shameful addictive habits that he will conceal.

Let the Custos be aware that the evil that remains in the darkness of his soul sows a secret, metastasizing, often (at least initially) externally unnoticed division in the married couple's relationship.

Spiritual Practice

Be Faithful to Your Marriage Vows

Whether you fall into financial, emotional, or sexual infidelity, make every effort to cease from the activity immediately. Remember that, in a mysterious way, because of your God-given authority, your sins and the consequences of them are transferred to your children. Seek a priest immediately and, if necessary, meet with a therapist. Often, immoral addictive behavior is the consequence of childhood wounds that have been buried rather than healed.

Rule 23

How the Custos Is to Oppose the False Spirit of Infidelity

The proverb says, "He who conceals his transgression will not prosper, but he who confesses and forsakes them will obtain mercy" (Prov. 28:13). Let the Custos understand that if he acts deceitfully or is concealing sinful behavior from his wife, it is essential that he first confess his sins sacramentally to a priest; second, seek spiritual counsel; third (if appropriate and if his confessor deems that it will not undermine his marriage), confess his sin to his wife; and fourth, ask her for forgiveness. By confessing his sin to and asking forgiveness from his wife, the Custos will be more likely to receive compassion. Let the Custos be aware that "nothing is hid that shall not be made manifest, nor anything secret that shall not be known and come to light" (Luke 8:17). Therefore, "confess your sins to one another, and pray one for another, that you may be healed" (James 5:16).

Spiritual Practice

BRING INFIDELITY TO LIGHT

If you have been or are unfaithful to your wife, meet with a priest as soon as possible. First, make the decision truly to repent of this sinful behavior. Second, confess your infidelity to a priest. Do not make excuses or blame your wife for your behavior. The sin is yours. Own it. Finally, ask your confessor whether you ought to disclose your infidelity to your wife. Be reconciled with God and trust that He will rebuild your marriage.

Section 5

Counsels Pertaining to the Custos' Relationship with God

Rule 1

The Custos' Need for Silence

If the soldier is to receive orders from his general for the purpose of being victorious in battle, or the beloved is to receive intimacies from her lover for the purpose of deepening unity, it is necessary in both cases that the receiver become attuned to the directives, counsels, and affirmations given by the initiator. In a similar manner, if the Custos is to be victorious in the spiritual battle, while also increasing always in union with God, it is necessary that he build his relationship with God on the foundation of silence. By intentionally allocating specific daily periods of silence in which he quiets the world's voices, cacophony, and false gospel and turns his gaze of attention upon His Divine Lord, the Custos becomes sensitive to God's presence — the God who expresses Himself by divine directives, counsels, signal graces, consolations, and delight and occasionally by spiritual darkness and aridity.

As it is written, "Sacrifice and offering thou dost not desire; but thou hast given me an open ear" (Ps. 40:6). A saying attributed to the Mystical Doctor, St. John of the Cross, is "God's first language is silence." It is in silence that God speaks, and it is without sound that His voice is heard. Let the Custos have confidence that the Word always speaks, but rarely does He find one willing to listen. Therefore, if the Custos is to be consistent in daily embracing silence with God, he will eventually become a good steward of God's varied grace (see 1 Pet. 4:10) and a mouthpiece for God.

Spiritual Practice

Gospel Reflection for Fifteen Minutes

First, identify a consistent time in which you can meet with Jesus Christ daily for fifteen minutes. At that time, enter your prayer place and invoke the Holy Spirit. Ask Jesus for two things: (1) that you may know Him (His character, His sentiments, His desires, His will) and (2) that you may become like Him. Then read the Gospel reading for Mass that day. Reflect on that Gospel passage, repeatedly asking Jesus, "What does this reveal about You?" Finally, respond by asking for the grace to become like Him.

Rule 2

The Evil Spirits' Intention to Deter the Custos from Embracing Silence

Let the Custos be aware that as God encourages and invites him to come into His presence by embracing silence, the evil spirits, on the contrary, will attempt to convince the Custos that he cannot be content or obtain joy — or, in some cases, that he cannot even survive — without the consistent stimulation of noise that tickles the ears; and that silence with God is torturous and difficult to endure for extended periods.

The evil spirits constantly discourage the Custos from embracing silence (for to embrace silence demands a certain amount of courage) while also offering the noises of the world (music, media stimulation, news sources, and the like) as an alternative enticement. As a soldier becomes incapable of hearing his general's directive due to the overwhelming noise caused by sounds of warfare, so the man who embraces the kingdom of noise, rejecting the invitation to embrace periods of silence with God, becomes incapable of discerning God's presence, directives, and counsel; he will eventually fail in his vocational mission. To impart the wisdom and charity of God to others, one must possess that divine wisdom and charity, and to possess these divine gifts demands that one allow himself to be possessed by God. This mutual possession occurs primarily by means of embracing silence with God. For, again, one cannot give what he does not possess.

Spiritual Practice

Evening Prayer for Fifteen Minutes

First, identify a consistent time in which you can meet with Jesus Christ daily for fifteen minutes. Second, enter your prayer place. Third, invoke the Holy Spirit. Use the events and the circumstances of the day, particularly your conversations with your wife and children, as the foundation of your meditation. Then, simply invite God into your life, asking Him for His guidance and blessing.

Rule 3

The Trust Demanded to Embrace Silence

Let the Custos understand that if he is to dedicate himself to embracing periods of silence with God daily and consistently, it is imperative that he have an unwavering trust in God, believing that the Word always speaks. Let the Custos also be aware that, even if he does not perceive God's voice, God is most generous in infusing the soul of the Custos with His divine presence while secretly supplying counsel and wisdom. Therefore, let the Custos be sensitive to the Holy Spirit's invitation to sacrifice courageously the voices and the stimulations of the world in exchange for silence with God. The more the Custos sacrifices audible delights in exchange for silence with God, the more God will supply him with His divine presence, counsel, and wisdom. For it is impossible that the generous God can be outdone in generosity.

Spiritual Practice

Abstain from Your Phone and Computer

Before your morning prayer and after your evening prayer, resist the temptation to use your phone. This will allow your mind to meditate on the things of God without distraction.

Rule 4

Two Reasons the Evil Spirits Discourage Silence

Although God is continually inspiring the Custos to sacrifice courageously the noises of the world in exchange for embracing silence with Him, the evil spirits, on the contrary, continually discourage and distract him from embracing silence with God. Let the Custos be aware that the evil spirits use two primary tactics to convince him to reject the divine invitation to silence. First, the evil spirits instill fear that God will not speak and that, therefore, the time spent in silence appears to be wasted, misused, or too great a sacrifice. Second, the evil spirits instill a fear that God will speak and direct the Custos to change his ways, to convert his life to God, to repent of evil habits, to reform his life, or to act charitably in ways that appear to be far too demanding. Though the noises of the world offer mental distraction and temporary false consolation, even these reasons for avoiding silence are founded upon the two primary deceptive reasons listed above. Let the Custos be aware that when he fears that God will not grant counsel or when he lacks trust in the goodness of God, the evil spirits are at hand, influencing him to resist the very power that empowers him to resist the evil spirits.

Spiritual Practice

Reduce All Forms of Media

To become capable of discerning the still, small voice of God, it is vital that the voices of the world be muted. Strive for periods of silence for the purpose of being attentive to divine impulses by silencing radio, music, news, and social media feeds. Dedicate this time, whether driving or sitting at home, to God. Initially, the silence may feel awkward, but eventually you will crave such moments of solitude, and in them, you will become capable of receiving divine counsel.

Rule 5

The Custos' Offering of His Firstfruits to God

The Custos is not a consecrated religious; rather, he exists "in the world." Because of this, he will be greatly challenged to establish daily, consistent, scheduled periods of prayer marked by the character of silence. From the moment he awakens, his duties, responsibilities, worldly distractions, and social engagements increase steadily and significantly. Considering this, the Custos will benefit greatly from rising early in the morning and dedicating the first portion of his day to God in prayer and silence. Bear in mind that during particular seasons of life, such as when he has an infant who consistently awakens in the very early hours, this might not be practical; in such cases, he might strive to set aside the first portion of the baby's morning naptime for prayer and silence. For as the Lord promises: "But seek first his kingdom and his righteousness, and all these things shall be yours as well" (Matt. 6:33). Justice toward God is to give Him what is due to Him. As it is written, "To know thee [God] is complete righteousness" (Wisd. 15:3). The holy Doctor gives this counsel to those who are not in religious life: "Set aside an hour every day before the midday meal, if possible, early in the morning, when your mind is less distracted and fresher after the night's rest. Don't extend it for more than an hour unless your spiritual director expressly tells you to do so."[7] Therefore,

[7] St. Francis de Sales, *An Introduction to the Devout Life*, pt. 2, chap. 1, no. 3.

let the Custos dedicate the firstfruits of his time and his day to God, trusting that God will grant all things necessary for his vocational state.

Spiritual Practice

Morning Offering

Begin each day by prostrating yourself before God the Father, offering to Him all that you are and all that you have, while also asking him:

Abba, Father, bless the work of my hands (see Ps. 90:17).

Rule 6

Primary Temptations to Resist a Life of Prayer

Let the Custos be aware that the evil spirits will assail him with feelings of fatigue, weariness, anxiousness for his labors and responsibilities, and, initially, apparently consoling distractions for the purpose of convincing him that he has not the time to pray, or, because he has perhaps been blessed temporally, that he has no need to pray. If the evil spirits cannot completely discourage him from embracing silence, they will attempt to lull him into spiritual slothfulness and procrastination for the purpose of delaying the moment he wakes in the morning, and thus delay his prayer. Again, the evil spirits' intent is that the Custos' prayer time will be minimized, rushed, shallow, or neglected altogether. An often-used tactic of the evil spirits is to entice the Custos to remain awake late in the evening, thus reducing his hours of sleep, which consequently increases the temptation to neglect morning prayer or decreases his ability to be attentive to God during that prayer time.

Let the Custos be aware that the evil spirits are bent on disrupting his daily prayer routine, which instills in him discouragement and a feeling of failure. The evil spirits will also attempt to convince him that, because he is tired, his prayers will be of no value; or that he ought not to reduce his sleep time for fear of illness or poor performance in his labors; or that he will be able to make up for the lost prayer time later in the day; or that there is too much godly labor that needs his attention and therefore his labors must commence immediately; or that he has what he needs and therefore has no need for prayer.

The evil spirits know that God highly regards and rewards the man who gives his firstfruits to Him and that God grants power in prayer, which makes the Custos a tremendous threat to the kingdom of evil.

✛

Spiritual Practice

Determine Your Times of Rising and Retiring

A man's prayer life depends on his prayer schedule. A man's prayer schedule depends on his sleeping schedule.

First, identify the number of hours of sleep you need. Second, identify the time at which you need to rise to pray, prepare for the workday, and commute to work. Third, determine your bedtime based on the hours of sleep you need. Finally, strive to maintain this schedule consistently. One of the keys to a thriving prayer life is consistency in one's schedule.

Rule 7

The Need to Begin Again Immediately

Let the Custos be aware that, when he fails in his attempts to offer the fruits of his time to God in prayer, or when he fails to meet with God at his scheduled prayer times, the evil spirits will assail him with the temptation to surrender his life of prayer. To fail does not indicate that one is a failure. Only he who fails to persevere is the one who becomes a failure. Therefore, let the Custos, after recognizing that he has failed in his duty to embrace silence with God, immediately turn to God in confidence, making a firm resolution to be faithful to his already established prayer commitments. God promises through the prophet, "Return to me, and I will return to you" (Mal. 3:7). And Our Lord Jesus promises that "him who comes to me, I will not cast out" (John 6:37). Again, Our Lord assures us, "How much more will the heavenly Father give the Holy Spirit to those who ask him!" (Luke 11:13).

Spiritual Practice

Determine and Commit to a Prayer Schedule

Identify those times during your waking hours in which you can pray. Because you are not a monastic, your prayer usually cannot be long in duration. Therefore, as a house typically rests on a foundation of four walls, those brief moments of prayer in your day will become "pillars" that hold up your "spiritual house."

For example:

Morning offering (30 seconds)
Decade(s) of the Rosary in preparation for morning meditation (7 minutes)
Morning prayer meditation on the Gospel (15 minutes)
Angelus (Noon — 45 seconds)
Chaplet of Divine Mercy (3 p.m. — 7 minutes)
Family prayer time (10 minutes)
Petitions with wife (5 minutes)
Evening prayer (5 minutes)
Evening examen (3 minutes)

Rule 8

False Humility

Let the Custos be aware that the evil spirits will tempt him to condemn himself for his failure to fulfill his spiritual commitments. Self-deprecation and self-condemnation will only further his discouragement. If the Custos succumbs to the temptation to wallow in guilt and self-pity rather than repent, his false pride will condition him to believe himself in a more tragic state than he is (beyond the aid and power of God). Therefore, let him immediately embrace his humiliation by repenting and making a firm resolution to amend his ways. If he does so, God will reward him with the virtue of humility, which will afford him the virtue of fortitude, thus affording him the courage to return to Him with wholehearted trust.

Spiritual Practice

Reaffirm Your Trust in Jesus Christ

Reaffirm your trust in Jesus Christ by praying the Chaplet of Divine Mercy at three o'clock.

Rule 9

Silence Before Men

In addition to embracing silence before God, the Custos is to embrace silence before men. Let the Custos be aware that human respect — that is, the desire to be respected, to receive recognition, to be honored and esteemed by men — is the curse of the ages; it weakens man's resolve to overcome sin and the flesh and the devil in his service of God. Silence before men quiets and subdues those prideful movements toward valuing and obtaining human respect and the glory that comes from men. For the Lord Jesus said, "I do not receive glory from men" (John 5:41); and after He multiplied the loaves and the fishes, and the crowds desired to make Him their king, Jesus fled to the silent hiddenness of the mountains to be in solitude with His Father. Let the Custos notice that our Lord's example highlights the true motivation for doing good works: to glorify the Father, not to receive the glory of men. As it is written, "It is better to take refuge in the Lord than to put confidence in princes" (Ps. 118:9).

Spiritual Practice

Prayer to Overcome the Desire for Human Glory

When you are assailed by feelings of inadequacy or the temptation to pursue vainglory, pray often:

Abba, Father, make me like St. Joseph — little, silent, and hidden. Amen.

Rule 10

Discerning Between the Motivation for Embracing Silence and the Consequence of It

Let the Custos understand that silence before men, therefore, concerns the intentionality of man's soul and not necessarily the consequence of this practice. There are men who do not receive glory from men and yet desire it greatly, which is sinful; and there are also men who do not desire the glory of men and receive it nonetheless, which is not sinful. The proper motivation and intention is determined by the Custos; the consequence is determined by God.

Therefore, let the Custos' intention always be in accordance with the prayer "Not to us, O Lord, not to us, but to thy name give glory" (Ps. 115:1). And again, heeding our Lord's command, "Seek not seats of honor," for the Pharisees "love the place of honor at feasts and the best seats in the synagogues" (Matt. 23:6); and Jesus warns, "Truly, I say to you, they have their reward" (Matt. 6:2). Those who live for the honors of men allow themselves to be sifted by the opinions of men, whereas those who live for the glory of God will be glorified by God and will rise above men's opinions of them.

Let the Custos heed the words of the holy apostle: "Whatever your task, work heartily, as serving the Lord and not men" (Col. 3:23). And again, we are reminded, "Obey in everything those who are your earthly masters, not with eyeservice, as men-pleasers, but in singleness of heart, fearing the Lord" (Col. 3:22). This simplicity, this purity of heart, is the pure motivation to glorify God alone, without any attempt to usurp His glory for oneself: "All flesh is like grass and all its glory like the flower of grass. The grass withers, and the flower falls" (1 Pet. 1:24). The Custos who considers the respect and honor of men to be grass that withers and is determined to glorify God — and not himself — will, by his life, be called "through our gospel, so that [he] may obtain the glory of our Lord Jesus Christ" (2 Thess. 2:14); for "he who began a good work in you will bring it to completion at the day of Jesus Christ" (Phil. 1:6).

Let the Custos never attempt to control the outcome of his decision to be silent before men. God alone will determine whether he be exalted or humbled in the sight of men, for it is written, "The LORD makes poor and makes rich; he brings low, he also exalts" (1 Sam. 2:7). Again, "For every one who exalts himself will be humbled, and he who humbles himself will be exalted" (Luke 14:11). As the holy prophet praises God, "Thou hast wrought for us all our works" (Isa. 26:12).

Spiritual Practice
MORNING OFFERING OF WORK

Allow part of your morning offering to be focused on your work for the day. First, offer your work and all that it entails to God. Second, ask God the Father to bless your work. Third, ask Him to give you the grace to honor Him by doing your work with excellence.

Rule 11

The Evil Spirits' Desire to Convince the Custos That He Needs Human Respect

Let the Custos be aware that whereas God inspires him not to seek the glory of men but, rather, to live to glorify God, the evil spirits, on the contrary, will lure and will use apparently logical reasoning — even Sacred Scripture — to convince the Custos to bring attention to himself in his efforts in order to glorify God or to use God and the things of God to bring glory to himself. For as the Lord Himself says, "Let your light so shine before men, that they may see your good works and give glory to your Father who is in heaven" (Matt. 5:16).

Our Lord also warns, however, that when performing good works, such as prayer, fasting, and almsgiving, one is to do these things in "secret; and your Father who sees in secret will reward you" (Matt. 6:6), rather than being like those who do such good works to bring attention to themselves.

Let the Custos be aware that to "let" his light shine is not to suppress the goodness of God that He intends to manifest in and through him. The evil spirits' desire to tempt or lead the Custos to make himself known to be good by his good works (which is self-exaltation) is contrary to God's will. Rather, the Custos is to allow the goodness of God to be expressed in and through himself.

Spiritual Practice

One Daily Hidden Sacrifice

Identify sacrifices that are in keeping with your vocational duties and personal health. Create a list of these that you can draw from with very little thought. Each morning, during your morning offering, decide which small hidden sacrifice you will offer to God. This sacrifice could be as little as not snacking between meals or as costly as not defending yourself when being ridiculed. Regardless, by emptying ourselves of our sensory attachments, God fills us more with His holy presence.

Rule 12

The Domestic Life's Ability to Purify the Custos' Intentions

The domestic life and the vocation of marriage and fatherhood are designed by God to be a purifying fire that burns away the dross of self-idolatry, vain ambitions, and self-exaltation. A man's wife and children know him as he truly is, more than the outside world knows him; they know his virtue and his vices; his strengths and his weaknesses; his fidelity and his infidelities. Considering this, the Custos stands before the members of his family in a state of spiritual nakedness. Yet let the Custos be consoled, for God allows this vulnerability as a means for his acquiring the virtue of humility. As the holy Doctor says, "We cannot be humble without self-knowledge."[8] A saying attributed to the Angelic Doctor, St. Thomas Aquinas, is "To know oneself is to see oneself as God sees us, and this is humility." And this saying is attributed to another Doctor, St. Francis de Sales: "The road to humility is paved with the sharp stones of humiliations." "He who is truly humble," says St. Bernard, "knows how to convert all his humiliations into humility."[9] Therefore, let the Custos see his vocation as a means for obtaining the foundation of all virtues: humility.

[8] St. Teresa of Ávila, *Interior Castle*, First Mansions, chap. 2.

[9] Quoted in the preface to Cajetan de Bergamo, *Humility of Heart*.

Spiritual Practice

Living the Spirit of Sacrifice

While offering sacrifices, mortification, and abnegations to God, avoid all grumbling, complaining, and boasting. Instead, secretly pray:

Abba, I offer this to You.

Rule 13

The Custos' Response to the Purification of His Desire for Human Recognition

The Custos lives in a state of vulnerability before his family, who know him as he truly is. He will respond to this vulnerability in one of three ways.

1. Not receiving honors and glory from his family members to the extent that he desires, he will pursue them in his labors, in vain ambitions, among his friendships and nonfamilial relationships, from sexual immorality, and even and sometimes especially, in religious pursuits, such as teaching and evangelization — to the neglect and detriment of his primary vocation. Yet, as one confessor said, "Do not become a streetlamp only for your house to go dark."
2. He will surrender the true and divine desire to achieve the glory of God and to live a life of greatness, and he will instead resort to living a tepid, slothful life, pursuing ease, comfort, and temporal consolations, which will lead his family into spiritual apathy and disdain for God's Fatherhood.
3. When not receiving honors — to the extent that he desires — from his wife and children, the Custos may embrace this humiliation as it truly is: divine providence, as coming from the hand of God; and receiving it as such, he will begin to walk humbly with the Lord (see Mic. 6:8) by applying himself to the service of his family, counting others as greater than himself.

By rejecting the desire for the respect of men and, rather, living in service of his family, the Custos will arrive at true self-knowledge, which is humility. By being humble, he will find that God will exalt him. But let the Custos be aware that if he becomes habituated to seeking the esteem of men or habituated to seeking escape from the arduous call to virtue, he will fail in the leadership of his family.

Spiritual Practice

Acts of Service That Aid the Family

The family has chores and duties that all its members can participate in. The father, by divine commission, is naturally and supernaturally understood as the spiritual leader. Therefore, identify acts of service you can do to help your family. For example, you could unload the dishwasher or help wash the dishes or clean the kitchen after dinner. You could put the little children to bed. Acts of service such as these will help you as the father to become the initiator of self-giving love. If you initiate, your family will follow your example of self-giving.

Rule 14

The Power That Sacrifice Gives to Prayer

Let the Custos be aware that if his prayer is to have a lasting, transformative effect and intercessory power, it is essential that it be animated by sacrifice. Sacrifices, mortifications, penances, and sufferings offered to God without complaint all demonstrate that the Custos' prayers are not merely lip service — which is a common characteristic of men's prayers in every generation. As the Lord says, "This people honors me with their lips, but their heart is far from me" (Matt. 15:8). Sacrifice, however, will help a man mean what he prays and will enable his prayer to be meaningful. And this is a reciprocal relationship, for prayer inspires one to sacrifice, and sacrifice animates the power of prayer. The body is made for sacrifice, and sacrifice is for the Body. Therefore, the Custos has been given a "holy priesthood, to offer spiritual sacrifices acceptable to God through Jesus Christ" (1 Pet. 2:5).

It is God who inspires and wills that the Custos offer such sacrifices that conform to his state of health, his vocation, and his mental well-being, so that he may be more fully united to Christ. For to suffer with Christ, who suffered for man, is to know Christ. God, who had no body and was incapable of suffering, assumed a body so that He might suffer for the Body, His Church. This is one reason God elevates redeemed man above the angels: angels, who do not have bodies, cannot suffer corporally. The human person can suffer in his body for the sake of the Body of Christ, in union with the sufferings of Christ's body. This is the Custos' dignity. As the holy apostle says, "It has been granted to you that for the sake of Christ you should not only believe in him but also suffer for his sake" (Phil. 1:29); and again, "Now I rejoice in my sufferings for your sake, and in my flesh I complete what is lacking in Christ's afflictions for the sake of his body, that is, the church" (Col. 1:24). Therefore, let the Custos offer corporal sacrifice daily, regardless of how small the offering may be, in union with his prayers.

Spiritual Practice

Fast Day

If spiritual fervor is manifest, and God calls a man to increase his self-offering, he can identify one day a week, or biweekly, on which to fast. A man must determine the intensity of his fast. For some it may be skipping a meal; for another, not eating throughout the day. Fasting is depriving oneself of food and drink. The man is to do this as an offering to God for the salvation and sanctification of his family. If the lack of food induces him to become unreasonably agitated, easily frustrated, or irritable, however, he should have the humility to recognize that, for the peace of his family, he should choose a different mortification; such instances are a sign that God is not calling him to this particular kind of sacrifice.

Rule 15

Two Ways the Evil Spirits Undermine the Intention to Sacrifice

Let the Custos be aware that as God inspires him to offer sacrifices for the purpose of more fully uniting himself with and conforming himself to Christ and also to bless his intercessory power, the evil spirits, on the contrary, tempt the Custos to offer sacrifices in two disordered ways. First, the evil spirits instill a pusillanimous fear into the Custos' soul, convincing him that he is not capable of undergoing certain inspired sacrifices; or that Jesus Christ has accomplished all by His "once for all" sacrifice (Heb. 10:10) and therefore there is no need for him to participate in presenting his body "as a living sacrifice, holy and acceptable to God" (Rom. 12:1); or that his sacrifice is too insignificant, and thus he excuses himself from this act of spiritual worship.

On the other hand, the evil spirits convince the Custos that he must maximize his sufferings for the purpose of proving his self-worth to himself and to God. This type of sacrifice amounts to self-justification, which God rejects. Let the Custos be aware that if he embraces this type of false spirituality, his religious service will be marked with rigor; idolatry of laws, disciplines, and traditions of men; harsh criticism, rash judgments, and severe condemnation of his fellow man; and a lack of real compassion for or understanding of the plight of other sinners. In this case, the supposed practice of the very religion that is intended to draw him firmly to God becomes a grave hindrance, which inevitably will repel his wife and children.

Spiritual Practice

Feast Days

The Church calendar offers the faithful many solemnities and feast days to rejoice in God, His Son, the Holy Spirit, Holy Mary, St. Joseph, and those individuals (the saints) whom God has glorified. First, review periodically the Church calendar and its upcoming feasts. Second, identify which feasts your family will celebrate. Third, on those days, intentionally celebrate with food, desserts, music, festivity, and prayer. By your doing so, your children will understand that religion consists not only of fasting but also of feasting — and that the fasting exists to prepare us for the feast.

Rule 16

Signs of True Prayer and Sacrifice

Let the Custos understand that the fruits of true prayer coupled with sacrifice is an increased love for God and his neighbor. If love for either is lacking, or is not increasing, the Custos' prayers, their form, their intention, and the manner in which he sacrifices must be examined for the purpose of determining why his prayers are not bearing the twofold mark of charity. As the apostle says, "If any one says, 'I love God,' and hates his brother, he is a liar; for he who does not love his brother whom he has seen, cannot love God whom he has not seen" (1 John 4:20). Increased love for his fellow man, together with an ardent desire to save sinners from damnation and a compassion for one's enemies, are indicators that one's prayer life is good and true.

Spiritual Practice

Examen Using the Beatitudes

Perhaps once a month, it is beneficial to examine one's conscience by using the Beatitudes (see appendix 2 for guiding questions). This offers us the ability to look at our spiritual life and leadership from a perspective that is framed not by "thou shalt nots" but by "thou shalts."

Section 6

Counsels Pertaining to the Custos' Fatherhood

Rule 1

He Whom the Human Father Represents

As an icon represents a transcendent reality or even God Himself, allowing the one who gazes upon it entrance into the sublime and heavenly realms, so also the human father is endowed by God with the power to be a living "icon," a human reflection of God the Father, to His children. As the holy pontiff said, the human father's mission is to reveal and reflect "the very fatherhood of God."[10] Our Lord Himself proclaims as much: "If you then, who are evil, know how to give good gifts to your children, how much more will your Father who is in heaven give good things to those who ask him!" (Matt. 7:11). Our Lord Jesus demonstrates here that the human father, even in his lowliness, expresses the mercy and glory of God the Father.

Therefore, let the Custos be aware of whom he is called to reveal and reflect. Without his perceiving it, his family studies his words and actions. He is a human lens through which they see and eventually understand — even minimally — the glory of God's Fatherhood.

[10] Pope John Paul II, *Familiaris Consortio* 25.

Spiritual Practice

Pray to Become Like God the Father

Pray often:

Abba, Father, make me like unto St. Joseph, a father on earth, that I may become like unto You, the Father in Heaven.

Rule 2

How the Evil Spirits Use the Human Father to Distort the Image of God the Father

As God has endowed the human father with the office and duty to reveal and reflect the divine Fatherhood of God, the evil spirits, on the contrary, make every attempt to distort and malign the image of the human father so that he may represent and reflect the image of the father of lies — while those looking on believe that this distorted image reflects the Divine Father.

Considering this, it is imperative that the Custos — with the help of God — intentionally labor to accomplish two things: (1) make it his aim and purpose to learn of and understand the true identity and characteristics of the Heavenly Father, which are always good, true, and merciful; and (2) place his trust completely and without reserve in this benevolent Father. For the evil spirits make every attempt to convince the human father that God has the devil's attributes and that the devil has God's attributes. That which the Custos believes he will live, and that which he lives will be learned by his children. If the Custos believes God is like the devil, his fatherhood will reflect that devilry, and his children will believe God is like the devil.

Spiritual Practice

Journal Reflection

Write three sentences describing your perception of God the Father. Be honest. Then write three sentences about the father you would like to be. Reflect on both and determine where the variance is — if there is one. Then ask God to reveal His true Fatherhood to you.

Rule 3

Three Primary Modes Through Which the Custos Expresses God's Fatherhood

Let the Custos understand that he reflects and reveals God's Fatherhood in three primary ways: (1) He is the visible face of the Divine Father, which his children are unable to see; (2) he is the audible voice of the Divine Father, which his children are unable to hear; and (3) he is the physical touch of the Divine Father, which his children are unable to feel.

Therefore, let the Custos be immersed in the Word of God, growing in knowledge of God's Fatherhood through the humanity of Christ. For it is Christ's humanity that expresses the fullness of the Deity bodily: "For in him the whole fulness of deity dwells bodily" (Col. 2:9), and it is by means of His Incarnation that God the Father's face, voice, and touch are revealed, as Christ Himself says: "He who has seen me has seen the Father" (John 14:9); and again, "Christ the power of God and the wisdom of God" (1 Cor. 1:24). If the Custos learns from Christ's example and follows it, his gaze toward his child will be loving: "And Jesus looking upon him loved him" (Mark 10:21); his words will be inspired: "For the Holy Spirit will teach you in that very hour what you ought to say" (Luke 12:12); and his touch will be appropriate and affirming: "Then children were brought to him that he might lay his hands on them and pray" (Matt. 19:13).

Spiritual Practice

One Daily Act of Affirmation and Encouragement to Your Child

First, reflect on aspects and characteristics that your child possesses that reflect God's goodness. (If your child is struggling behaviorally, this could be challenging.) Second, verbally affirm your child for those good characteristics or behaviors. Even if the child has fulfilled a duty that is incumbent upon him or her, such as taking out the trash, thank the child. Last, try to see your child anew — through your own childhood, how you used to behave. Recall God's patience with you. Then perhaps you will more readily see your child's sense of humor, beauty, hard work, or physical abilities. Regardless, be intentional about affirming your child daily.

Rule 4

The Evil Spirits' Usurpation of These Three Modes

Let the Custos be aware that as God wills and appoints the human father to express the divine Fatherhood by means of the three primary modes, the evil spirits, on the contrary, will attempt to usurp those modes, misusing them as expressions of the father of lies.

First, the evil spirits will tempt the father to misuse his gaze by looking upon his child with disappointment, dissatisfaction, or contempt; or by looking upon his child in a vicarious manner, as an object or means for his own personal fulfillment, or as a servant or slave, or, in extreme and perverted cases, as an object of lust and personal sexual gratification. On the other hand, the evil spirits will assail the Custos with a sense of personal shame due to his infidelities and sins, thereby conditioning him to avoid eye contact with his child; or to begin resenting his child, for when he looks upon his child's innocence, he is reminded of his guilt; or to neglect gazing upon his child altogether because he begins to believe that he is incapable of transmitting God's love.

Second, the evil spirits will tempt the Custos, on one hand, to use his voice in a harsh, demeaning, biting, and nagging manner that conditions the child to despair of his own goodness; or, on the other hand, will tempt him to use flattery and manipulative words to coerce the child. Additionally, the demons will tempt the Custos to refrain from using words of affirmation, charity, discipline, protection, guidance, and encouragement, due to the hardening of his heart, which closes him off from receiving encouragement from God his Father.

Third, the evil spirits will tempt the Custos to misuse the expression of touch, through physical force, by inflicting unnecessary pain, believing that physical abuse is how a father is to "control" his child; or, on the other hand, by avoiding all physical discipline for fear of harming the child psychologically and emotionally. Additionally, the evil spirits will tempt the Custos to neglect to touch his child affirmatively and appropriately for fear of vulnerability and awkwardness, or, in extreme cases, to touch the child in an inappropriate, disordered, and perverted manner. Let the Custos be aware that all of the above are certain indicators that he is not reflecting and transmitting the benevolent, loving fatherhood of God to his child, but rather, he has allowed himself to become a channel of the father of lies.

Spiritual Practice

One Daily Act of Physical Affection Toward Your Child

We are not spirits. We are bodily creatures. The body expresses the soul. To express the love we have for our children, it is imperative that we show them physical affection. Identify types of proper affection: hugs, kisses, pats on the back. Second, show those signs of affection daily. Third, don't overdo it. Regarding sons, remember that they instinctually love roughhousing. This also is a sign of affection and attention.

Rule 5

The Ultimate Purpose of Fatherhood

Let the Custos understand that a father's ultimate purpose is to aid his child, with the help of his wife, to become a saint. Therefore, it is imperative that the Custos identify his child as a temple of God and assist his child in his or her recognition of this divine indwelling. As the holy apostle says, "Do you not know that your body is a temple of the Holy Spirit within you?" (1 Cor. 6:19).

Therefore, all rules of God are at the service of fostering a trusting, loving relationship with God. Rules without a relationship distort religion into a false god, for they are attempts to justify oneself before God. As the holy apostle says, "No man is justified before God by the law" (Gal. 3:11).

Let the Custos heed the Lord's command: "Whoever receives one such child in my name receives me" (Matt. 18:5). Let the Custos understand that the more a father receives his child as Christ, the more the child will be receptive to receiving Christ. Therefore, let the Custos be intentional in acknowledging that his child is a temple of the Holy Spirit.

Spiritual Practice

Daughter Dates and Son Time

Our children want to know that they are chosen and desired. Daughter dates and son time signal to them that they are more important than a father's work or hobbies.

First, identify a day and time to spend with your child. Second, choose an activity that both of you like that is not complicated. For example, consider taking a son or daughter out for a treat (ice cream when they are younger, for example, or coffee when they are older) or for breakfast regularly or taking your son or daughter to the hardware store. Consistency is the key. Lastly, during that time, refrain from criticizing your child's academics and behavior. Simply try to have a good conversation and learn about your child. Over time, this builds incredible trust and rapport.

Rule 6

The Disordered Concept of "Being a Saint"

Let the Custos be aware that the evil spirits distort the concept of "being a saint" into "replicating" or "imitating" an idealistic version of a person canonized by Holy Mother Church. This false idealism, if left unchecked, can eclipse or, in some cases, extinguish the unique unrepeatability of the child and God's will to manifest His glory through the child in His predetermined manner. The evil spirits propose the idea of sainthood as a picture of personal glory and personal perfection; they suggest religion and its practices and devotions as means to be recognized, respected, and honored by men, but this receives the harshest condemnation from our Lord (see Matt. 6:2, 5, 16; 23:1–7).

Let the Custos understand, believe, and communicate to his child that "to be a saint" is to be a disciple of Christ, to trust God the Father, to fulfill the Heavenly Father's will, and, by means of the Cross — that is, by giving oneself for the glory of God — ultimately to live in the unity of the self-giving love of the triune God. The Christian's goal is never to glorify himself but to be drawn into the self-giving communion of the Persons of the Holy Trinity. To be a saint is to love, for it is by love that man is judged (see Matt. 25:31–46). Therefore, all efforts of the Custos are to foster and encourage true, deep communion between his children and God.

Spiritual Practice

Lead a Prayer of Thanksgiving at Meals

As the father and spiritual leader of your family, begin each meal with a prayer of thanksgiving to God the Father for His provision and protection. This demonstrates your dependence on, trust in, and gratitude to God the Father and also teaches your children how to be grateful to God. During mealtime, foster an atmosphere of charitable and joyful discussion. This bonds the family to one another and to God.

Rule 7

How the Evil Spirits Use the Lives of the Saints to Instill Fear

Let the Custos be aware that as God elevates and brings attention to the lives of particular saints for the purpose of inspiring His children to follow their example, the evil spirits, on the contrary, use the virtuous examples and heroic deeds of the saints as a means to instill a certain feeling of inferiority, anxiousness, and unhealthy pressure on the father because his child is not growing in or aspiring to sanctity as fast as he would like. By applying this pressure, the evil spirits condition the Custos to live in fear of his child's lack of spiritual progress, and because of this, he will become — supposedly in the name of God — demanding, legalistic, rigid, and repressive. And because he is meant to be an image of God, if the Custos succumbs to this temptation, his child will likely grow to resent religion and to perceive Jesus as oppressive, legalistic, and domineering, rather than merciful, charitable, joyful, forgiving, and patient. Additionally, if the child exerts signs of rebellion or resentment toward his father's expression of discipleship, the Custos, who is conditioned by this fear, will apply more pressure and will use God's law and God Himself as a means to guilt and pressure his child to repent of his or her ways. This pressure will not only exacerbate the relationship between God and the child but can instill a deep-seated resentment, if not hatred, toward God and eventually toward the human father. The feeling or sentiment "I must make my child a saint" or "I must ensure that my child become a saint" is a certain sign that the evil spirits are at work. For God alone sanctifies. As the exorcist says, "Self-reliance leads to self-hatred" (Msgr. John Essef).

Spiritual Practice

Pray Specifically for Each Child

During your morning offering, picture each child in your mind, and pray specifically for their sanctification and daily needs. If needed, have photos of them available to help you focus on them.

Rule 8

Two Laws That Aid a Father in Overcoming Anxiety Regarding His Child's Spiritual Advancement

Let the Custos understand that if he is to rise above the anxiety and pressure associated with his child's spiritual advancement or lack thereof, it is imperative that he live by the law of gradualness and the law of attraction. The law of gradualness is founded upon the knowledge that, during his short life, the Custos has achieved a certain level of sanctity, but he is nevertheless still inclined toward vice; yet, when evaluating his child's sanctity through his own degree of sanctity, he expects his child's spiritual life to be at his level. This expectation, however, is unfair and unrealistic. Therefore, with this understanding in mind, the Custos ought to adopt a spirit of patience, for "the Lord ... is forbearing toward you, not wishing that any should perish, but that all should reach repentance" (2 Pet. 3:9). The Custos should understand that faith and trust in God are proven by tests and sufferings and that his child has not encountered such trials as he himself has. For it is written that "through many tribulations we must enter the kingdom of God" (Acts 14:22). The Custos should abide patiently by the law of gradualness, never forcing his child's spiritual advancement.

The law of attraction mandates that a father's religious practices and beliefs be marked with the character of joy, patience, mercy, and, most of all, charity. The law of attraction expresses that religion is always at the service of the relationship between God and man and that it is in this relationship that the Custos takes great delight. If the Custos delights in his Heavenly Father and lives in friendship with Jesus Christ, his child will more likely be attracted not only to his human father but, by means of the association between his human father and the Heavenly Father, to his Father in Heaven also. For God promised that, through the prophet, He "will turn the hearts of fathers to their children and the hearts of children to their fathers" (Mal. 4:6); and again, our Lord Jesus commanded, "Let the children come to me, and do not hinder them; for to such belongs the kingdom of heaven" (Matt. 19:14).

Let the Custos understand that if he intentionally lives by these two laws, his child will find it easier to embrace the love of God and to choose to live for Him.

Spiritual Practice

Weekly Family Night

Family night is an evening dedicated to being with one another. This can be accomplished by playing games, sitting together and talking, going for a walk, watching a movie together, or any number of like things. Regardless of the particular activity, family night is a context that provides bonding experiences that are not religious per se.

First, choose the night of the week for family night. Second, as a family, identify things that you would all like to do together. Be consistent in spending this time with the family each week. In a sense, attendance is required. This is also a friendly context, so friends can be invited.

Rule 9

The Child's Essential Need for Discipline

Let the Custos understand that discipline is essential in helping his child grow in virtue and sanctity. "For the Lord disciplines him whom he loves, and chastises every son whom he receives. It is for discipline that you have to endure. God is treating you as sons; for what son is there whom his father does not discipline? If you are left without discipline, in which all have participated, then you are illegitimate children and not sons" (Heb. 12:6–8). The purpose of this discipline is to foster the Custos' child in the discipleship of Christ and therefore to assist him in becoming a true, perfected child of the Father. Therefore, the Custos' expression of discipline is to have the characteristics of the Heavenly Father's discipline: regulated, restrained, patient, and applied with tenderness and mercy. In each act of discipline, the Custos is to communicate to his child, in some manner, that the reason for the discipline is that he loves his child and does not desire that his child become a child of the world, the flesh, and the devil. Let the Custos be aware that if he does not discipline his child, the world most certainly will.

Spiritual Practice

How to Respond on the Next Occasion for Correction

Discipline makes the disciple. Discipline without love is abuse. Love without discipline is neglect. After your child's next act of disobedience, first pause and resist reacting. Second, be intentional about responding rationally — not emotionally. Third, communicate to your child the consequence (form of punishment). Finally, after the punishment is completed, sit down with your child, make good eye contact, and explain why that behavior is not acceptable.

The essence of what a father ought to communicate to his child is this: "Do you think I enjoy punishing you? No. I hate it. However, I love you enough to want the best for you. I want you to be happy and virtuous. If I don't correct you, you could grow up to be an adult brat whom the world will correct according to its own essentially disordered maxims."

Rule 10

The Evil Spirits' Two Temptations Regarding Discipline

Let the Custos be aware that the evil spirits will tempt him in two ways regarding the discipline of his child. One way is to tempt him to love his child without discipline, which is actually not love but a form of neglect of the child. If the Custos neglects to discipline with love, often the child will grow to become self-centered, lacking self-control, immoral, licentious, wanting in virtue, and unable to persevere amid trials and sufferings and will fail to comprehend consequences associated with his actions. Additionally, the child will fail to be responsible for himself and for others and will lack the Spirit of God, which is always self-giving.

The evil spirits will also tempt the Custos to discipline without love. This form of discipline lacks compassion, mercy, tenderness, and forgiveness and is exacting in judgment, harsh with verbal reprimands, and cruel in physical punishment. True discipline is always animated by charity and leads the child to become charitable. Vengeance, retaliation, venting hostility, and vociferousness are all certain signs that the evil spirits are influencing the Custos' expression of discipline.

Spiritual Practice

Assess Your Disciplinary Behavior

During a date night or a time when tensions are not high or a child has not misbehaved, ask your wife in what ways you could be a better disciplinarian. Do your best to receive her critique without deflecting, making excuses, or blaming others. Pray about her counsel. Then implement those disciplinary behavioral changes that, with her input, you have deemed necessary to being a father worthy of respect.

Rule 11

The Good Example of the Custos to His Child

As a master tradesman patiently and gradually trains his apprentice to become proficient, so also a Custos, by means of familial labor, serving his neighbor, humble example during social gatherings, conversations during meals, and his utmost respect for his wife and for all women, gradually trains his child in the ways of the Gospel. This demands that the Custos not only immerse himself in the Gospel of Jesus Christ but also that he embodies it in all circumstances of his life; for especially when the Custos is not aware that he is teaching, his child is learning from his outward example. Let the Custos understand that how a man prays is reflected in what he believes, and what he believes is reflected in how he acts, and how he acts is how he is perceived. Therefore, let the Custos reflect daily upon the Divine Word — that is, the Sacred Scripture — so that he may become a living word of God from which his child learns.

Spiritual Practice

Work Alongside Your Child

Identify those chores, projects, or duties that you or your child perform regularly; then identify ways that you can work alongside your child. This demonstrates your humility, a good work ethic, and familial solidarity.

An effective way to actualize this is by having a weekly family work time. Perhaps on Saturday morning, the family can work around the house, cleaning or accomplishing particular projects. By working with your child in this context, you show your child how to be a gift rather than a hireling.

Rule 12

The Custos' Good Example in Asking His Child for Forgiveness

Let the Custos be aware that if his discipline of his child is too harsh or demanding; if he misuses his power, his face, his voice, or his touch in an ungodly way — that is, in a manner that does not transmit the Divine Fatherhood of God to his child — he is to humble himself by asking his child to forgive him. By acting in this most humble manner, the Custos teaches his child what is perhaps the most important joint lesson: forgiveness and humility. As the apostle says, "Humble yourselves therefore under the mighty hand of God, that in due time he may exalt you" (1 Pet. 5:6). And again, our Lord Jesus commands us, "So if you are offering your gift at the altar, and there remember that your brother has something against you, leave your gift there before the altar and go; first be reconciled to your brother, and then come and offer your gift" (Matt. 5:23–24). It is said, "The fruit does not fall far from the tree"; thus, a child will bear the fruit of humility and forgiveness that his father often embodies.

Spiritual Practice

Ask Your Child for Forgiveness

When you hurt your child, immediately claim your offense. Then sincerely apologize by asking for forgiveness. Do not blame your child for your behavior. Finally, hug your child, assuring him or her of your love.

Rule 13

The Custos's Priestly Sacrifice of Thanksgiving

Let the Custos understand that, as priest of his family, he must ensure that his family consistently gathers for dinner in a spirit of thanksgiving. By means of his labor, he provides for the meal, gathers his family around these provisions, and leads them in a prayer of gratitude to Almighty God, who has generously provided. This priestly expression helps the children to embrace a Eucharistic way of life — that is, one of thanksgiving. As the psalmist prays, "He who brings thanksgiving as his sacrifice honors me" (Ps. 50:23). And again, "Offer to God a sacrifice of thanksgiving, and pay your vows to the Most High; and call upon me in the day of trouble; I will deliver you, and you shall glorify me" (Ps. 50:14–15).

Spiritual Practice

Nightly Family Thanksgiving Prayer

Toward the end of the day, first, gather your family together for a thanksgiving prayer. Second, begin by making the Sign of the Cross. Third, in your role as the father, express to God the Father your gratitude for several things. Fourth, prompt each member of your family to do likewise in turn. Last, as the father, close with a prayer.

Rule 14

The Necessity of Family Dinner

Let the Custos understand that the evil spirits will gradually condition his family to a life of busyness, numerous events, an overwhelming number of responsibilities, and employment demands that continually conflict with the gathering of the family around the dinner table. If the Custos allows this dynamic to persist, his family bond in Christ will be fragmented, the spirit of true thanksgiving nearly vanquished, his ability to know his children will become limited, and his godly influence over them largely compromised. Again, if the Custos does not make family dinner a daily priority, then the gathering of his family at the Sacred Meal of God the Father — that is, the Holy Sacrifice of His Son's Body and Blood as the Bread of Life — will not be a priority among the members of his family. There is a profound connection and correlation between the attendance of the family at the human father's table and the attendance and spirit of the family at the Table of God the Father, the altar of Jesus Christ. Therefore, let the Custos gather his family around his table daily — and, if not daily, as much as possible — so that his family may be gathered around the Altar of the Lord.

Spiritual Practice

Family Dinner

First, make family dinner a priority. This will demand compromises and sacrifices. Second, identify the optimal number of nights a week that you deem family dinner necessary. For some families, it is every night, as in former generations. For other families, only three nights a week may be possible. Regardless, identify the nights that family dinner is mandatory. Third, as the father and spiritual leader, begin each meal with a prayer of thanksgiving to God the Father for His provision and protection. This demonstrates your dependence on, trust in, and gratitude to God the Father and also teaches your children to be grateful to God. Finally, create an atmosphere of charitable and joyful discussion. This bonds the family to one another and to God.

Rule 15

How and Where the Custos Receives God's Power

Let the Custos know that God wills that he receive a significant portion of grace through the sacraments, particularly the Eucharist and Confession. The resurrected life of Christ, transmitted through these holy sacraments, empowers the Custos to become a reflection of God the Father, a holy temple through whom the Holy Spirit continually manifests His glory. The more a father becomes dependent on the sacraments, the more dependable he will be as a representative of God's Fatherhood to his wife and children. Therefore, God the Father will allow the human father to become ever more aware of his personal neediness, his limitations, and his weaknesses in order for him to become more dependent on Christ; and the more dependent the Custos is upon Christ and His sacraments, the greater the power of Christ will be manifested through him. For Jesus says, "Apart from me you can do nothing" (John 15:5) and "Abide in me" (John 15:4); "my grace is sufficient for you, for my power is made perfect in weakness" (2 Cor. 12:9); therefore, let the Custos not only be aware of his weaknesses and limitations but glory in them, so that by his being dependent on God, especially on the sacraments, the power of Christ may rest upon him (see 2 Cor. 12:9).

Spiritual Practice

Take Your Children to Morning Holy Mass and Confession on First Saturdays

The first Saturday of each month is traditionally the day on which the faithful make reparation to Our Blessed Mother for the sacrileges, injustices, and blasphemies against her Immaculate Heart. Devotion to Our Lady secures graces, sanctification, and salvation for the believer.

As the father of the family, tell your children, "Tomorrow we will be going to Mass and Confession together." Afterward, if possible, associate the experience with something fun or social, such as a big family breakfast. This creates a connection between God and joy. Finally, consecrate each of your children to Our Blessed Mother. Simply give them to her care.

Rule 16

Signs That the Custos Is Becoming Self-Reliant

Let the Custos understand that, as God summons him to become more aware of his neediness, weaknesses, and limitations, he must depend all the more fully on Christ and the grace He offers through the sacraments; the evil spirits, on the contrary, will tempt the father to believe that he is self-reliant, a man of sound reason and that the sacraments are merely empty, symbolic rituals and that therefore he has little or no need for them. The evil spirits will condition the Custos to believe that he must accomplish things by means of his own power. If the Custos distances himself from reliance on Jesus Christ and His sacraments, it is a certain sign that he has become self-reliant and, being self-reliant, will find that the vocation of leading his family to God and to Heaven will be greatly hindered. In fact, his self-reliance could become an idol that he unwittingly worships; by such worship, he will teach his children likewise, thus robbing them of the only power that can save their souls. Sadness or anger at his own failures, errors, and shortcomings; habitual perfectionism; and the inability to wait patiently for the Lord in times of distress are signs that the Custos is becoming or has become self-reliant.

Spiritual Practice

Poverty of Spirit

To combat self-reliance, we must become aware of our poverty. A beggar who has not eaten for days is pleased to eat a scrap of bread. When prideful, we believe ourselves entitled to more. We fail to remember that all is a gift from God.

Therefore, proclaim that all the good you possess is a gift from God. Rather than complaining that you do not have more, accept and rejoice in what you have been given. When you begin to accept what you have with gratitude, you will see that self-reliance and pride diminish while joy increases.

Rule 17

The Custos' Character of Charity

Let the Custos understand that the greatest lesson he can offer his child is his example of heroic sacrificial love. Christ's sacrifice has a magnetic quality that perpetually draws souls to union with Him. A father who leads by serving teaches his children the essence of leadership and how to lead: by self-gift, self-donation. To the degree that the Custos initiates and establishes this practice of self-giving love, his family will desire to serve Christ. The Custos' family and their willingness to serve, particularly other members of the family, will reflect his own self-donation. Often, the degree and intensity of his family's willingness to serve one another can help him gauge the effectiveness of his own leadership. If his children serve without coercion, or attempt to "outdo" others sincerely in service, the Custos is certainly establishing a pace of self-giving love. If his children resist serving, however, or lack a vision of charity and habitually resort to ease, comfort, and slothfulness, let the Custos examine himself to determine if he is setting an example of spiritual slothfulness or if he is setting a pace of self-giving love. For as the holy apostle says, "Love one another with brotherly affection; outdo one another in showing honor" (Rom. 12:10).

Spiritual Practice

Initiate Self-Donation

The next time your child needs assistance, rather than waiting for your wife or another child to help, step in and do it yourself. Initiate self-donation.

Rule 18

Two Disordered Forms of Leadership

Let the Custos be aware that as God wills that he consistently set the pace of self-giving love, the evil spirits, on the contrary, will make every attempt to lead him to one of two polarized leadership extremes. On the one hand, the evil spirits will induce him to dominate his children using the tactics of coercion, manipulation, bribery, and fear to obtain the desired responses from them. In this dynamic, children learn to view themselves as slaves of their father's will rather than the objects of their father's love. On the other hand, the evil spirits will attempt to convince the father to abdicate his role, removing his children's moral and familial responsibilities, minimizing the necessity for the children to be obedient to his authority. When the Custos surrenders his God-given authority out of fear of appearing to be domineering, he will inevitably condition his children to become self-focused, to be dominated by immorality, and to assume very little responsibility for their actions. The Custos' domestic church will lack order, and because of this lack of order, it will lack God's peace.

As the philosopher said, "The virtues stand in the middle."[11] Therefore, let the Custos not dominate his children with his authority or neglect the use of this authority but, rather, draw his children to his side, working closely with them, having sincere conversations with them, and intentionally choosing to spend time with them. By the father's doing so, the children will respond naturally to his

[11] "In medio stat virtus" (Aristotle).

authority. For if the Custos respects his children, the children will more likely to respect the Custos. If children believe that their father desires to invest in them, they are far more likely to respect the authority that their father embodies.

Spiritual Practice

Be the Face of God the Father to Your Child

When your child is trying to converse with you, stop, look into his or her eyes, and listen. If necessary, tell yourself that this moment with your child is more important than anything else that you might be doing. This demonstrates respect. A child who is respected by his father will learn to respect himself.

Rule 19

How the Custos' Perception of God Influences His Disposition Toward His Child

Let the Custos understand that the human father's perception of God the Father shapes the lived expression of his own fatherhood. If the Custos believes that God is generous, this divine generosity will be reflected in his fatherhood. If he believes that God is merciful and forbearing, these qualities will be reflected in his fatherhood, and so forth. In other words, if the Custos' relationship with God the Father is filial (that of a son who trusts his Father) and not servile (that of a slave toward his Master), then filial tenderness, patience, meekness, and charity will be expressed and reflected through his fatherhood. If, however, the Custos' perception is that God is rigid, demanding, domineering, non-benevolent, tending toward wrath, distant, or any other qualities like these, then these characteristics will be reflected in his own fatherhood — precisely by his being a domineering, rigid father or an indulgent, dismissive father. Remember Christ's parable of the wicked, slothful servant: The slothful servant's distorted perception of the master determined his fate (see Matt. 25:14–30). The human father's actions can become a lens through which he is able to evaluate his own relationship with God the Father. Let the Custos be aware that how he acts toward and reacts to his children is closely associated with how he perceives the Heavenly Father's disposition toward himself.

Spiritual Practice

Be Surprisingly Generous to Your Child

Occasionally, for no specific reason — not for anything good that the child has done — give your child a treat, perhaps something you could purchase on your way home from work. This will demonstrate, first, that you were thinking of your child; second, that you love your child; and finally, that you are an expression of God the Father's lavish generosity, which is not based on quid pro quo. This wins children for God the Father.

Rule 20

The Right and Duty of the Custos to Bless His Child

According to a saying commonly attributed to the holy Doctor St. Augustine, the human father is the "bishop of his home." Therefore, let the Custos understand and believe that God has endowed him with the power to be a "steward of God's varied grace" (see 1 Pet. 4:10). This distribution of grace is transmitted visibly and particularly by means of the blessing that the Custos gives his child daily. This blessing consists of calling upon God to grant His favor, protection from evil, and blessing on his child in the name of the Father, and of the Son, and of the Holy Spirit. This is his sacred duty and right.

Spiritual Practice

Bless Your Child

In the moment that you bless your child, you become the face of the Father, which your child cannot see; the voice of the Father, which your child cannot hear; and the touch of the Father, which your child cannot feel. First, identify the time of day that you will consistently bless your child. Second, trace the Sign of the Cross on your child's forehead while invoking God's blessing upon the child. Afterward, hug or kiss your child.

Example blessing:

> *May the Lord bless you and keep you. May His face shine kindly upon you. May the Lord grant you His kindness and peace. May God the Father bless you with His grace and favor, protect you from all evil, and allow you to behold His face for all eternity. Amen.*

Rule 21

The Custos' Ability to Be a Distributor of God's Manifold Grace

Let the Custos be aware that as God wills the human father to transmit His grace and blessing to his children, the evil spirits, on the contrary, will make every attempt to hinder or block the father from being a conduit of grace. The evil spirits will attempt to instill fear, embarrassment, or a sense of unworthiness in the mind of the Custos for the purpose of deterring him from blessing his children. Additionally, the demons will make every attempt to lure the father to consent to mortal sin. If the Custos persists in habitual sin without repenting, his ability to transfer grace will be hindered, if not altogether blocked, like a dam that holds back a river.

Being aware of his spiritual state (being either in a state of grace or in a state of mortal sin — though one cannot have absolute certitude regarding his spiritual state, nevertheless he must strive to be in the state of grace), the Custos can be confident as to whether he is transmitting grace to his child or not. If he is not, it is imperative that he sacramentally confess his sins and receive absolution. By doing so, he will allow God to restore his ability to be a channel of grace for his family. Once forgiven of his sins, the Custos has no need to fear that he is blocking the transmission of God's grace.

Spiritual Practice

Weekly Confession

If you sense that you are under siege, assailed by temptation and trials, go to Confession once per week. Exorcists have said that Confession is more powerful than an exorcism. Whereas an exorcism removes a demon, the Sacrament of Confession fills one with God's grace and presence.

Rule 22

Why the Custos Loves His Child

As God loves His children not for what they produce or for how they perform but simply because they are His — that is, because they are created by Him and for Him (see Col. 1:16) — in a similar manner, the Custos is to love his child not for what the child does or does not do but because the child is his child. He loves his child so that his child may experience the love of God the Father and so that, by experiencing that love, the child would desire to love God above himself and would desire Heaven.

Spiritual Practice

Assure Your Children of Your Love

Words of affirmation are powerful and influence a child. Tell your children often that you love them. Additionally, find an occasion, perhaps weekly, in which you can tell your children individually that you are thankful that they are your sons and daughters. This can be accomplished simply by saying things such as:

"Do you know I love you?"

"I am so thankful that you are my daughter."

"I am so proud of you."

Rule 23

The Custos' Unconditional Love for His Child

Let the Custos be aware that the evil spirits will attempt to lead the father to love his child more when his child performs, achieves, pleases, or produces well; and to love his child less when the child underachieves, fails, disappoints, or rebels. At the heart of both sinful tendencies is the Custos' subconscious or conscious erroneous and selfish intention to live vicariously through his child. To love a child more when one is pleased with the child or to love the child less when one is disappointed in the child does not image God the Father's love for His children; rather, it is the image of the father of lies. Let the Custos remember always that the father of the prodigal son had compassion on him, ran out to him, and meeting him, fell on his neck and kissed him (see Luke 15:11–32). Likewise, this same father also went out to his self-righteous son and said, "All that is mine is yours." Let the Custos understand from this account that God the Father's love is unconditional. As the psalmist says, "The Lord is merciful and gracious, slow to anger and abounding in steadfast love" (Ps. 103:8). The only condition that God requires of man is that he respond with love to divine love. For his part, let the Custos have an unconditional love for his child, and let him respect his child's freedom to respond to that love.

Spiritual Practice

What to Communicate When Disciplining Your Child

Never demean your child. Do not refer to your child as "stupid" or "good for nothing" or say anything such as "You always screw up" and the like.

On the next occasion when your child acts improperly, communicate to him or her, after having exercised the proper discipline, something to the effect of the following:

Do you think I love you less when you do wrong?

I may be disappointed in you, but my love for you never changes.

Do you think I love you more when you do well?

I may be proud of you, but my love for you is constant.

By communicating this, you are representing God the Father, who loves all of His children, regardless of their sins or achievements.

Section 7

Counsels Pertaining to the Custos' Work

Rule 1

The Goodness of Work

Let the Custos understand that his work, or human labor, is a gift from God, a participation in God's dominion over creation, a participation with God in establishing and maintaining right order, a participation in God's creativity, and a means to develop solutions that better mankind's living condition while also affording the Custos a means to provide temporally for his family. This participation is exemplified in the wedding in Cana, when Christ commands the servants to fill the jars with water that He will turn into wine (see John 2). The servants fill the jars to the brim, which indicates that they work with excellence. Yet it is Christ who transforms their labors — their water — into wine. This speaks of the divine will that God and man be partners in work. The Custos' labors exist to increase his confidence and competence while also, and more important, fostering a continual reliance on God; for, as the psalmist prays, "Let the favor of the Lord our God be upon us, and establish thou the work of our hands upon us, yea, the work of our hands establish thou it" (Ps. 90:17). Therefore, let the Custos do his work with excellence, rejoicing and being thankful for his labors and that he is able to labor; but also, let him continually ask that God direct and bless the work of his hands. By doing these three things, the Custos becomes a partner with God in his labors.

Spiritual Practice

Giving God Thanks

Give 10 percent of your income to the Church or to the less fortunate.

Rule 2

Two Ways That the Evil Spirits Will Distort the Goodness of Work

Let the Custos be aware that as God wills that work be a partnership between the creature and his Creator, the evil spirits, on the contrary, will use work to separate man from God and from his vocation in two primary ways. First, the evil spirits will tempt the Custos to believe that work is all toil, that it is merely an irksome burden and nothing more than a way to earn a wage, and that the ideal life is one that is free from labor. As "proof" that God created work to be burdensome, the demons will echo God's words: "In the sweat of your face you shall eat bread till you return to the ground" (Gen. 3:19). This attitude produces in the Custos an interior slothfulness or resistance or an eventual resentfulness toward labor, and it disposes him to seek not greater aspirations but the comforts and the idleness of the world and the flesh. Second, the evil spirits will tempt the Custos to believe that work is of such great value that it is the highest priority and the greatest necessity. This attitude creates a subconscious belief that the Custos' identity is derived primarily, if not solely, from his occupation. Let the Custos remember that he is defined not by what he does for a living but, rather, by those for whom he is living. One's occupations are transient, whereas one's vocation, the gift and call from God, is permanent and irrevocable (see Rom. 11:29). As the holy pontiff says, "Along with the humanity of the Son of God, work too has been taken up in the mystery of the Incarnation, and has also been redeemed in a special way. At the workbench where he plied his trade together with Jesus, Joseph brought human work closer to the mystery of the Redemption."[12]

Spiritual Practice

Work for God

During your morning offering, ask God the Father to grant you His Spirit so that you may do your work for Him with excellence.

[12] Pope John Paul II, apostolic exhortation *Redemptoris Custos* (August 15, 1989), no. 22.

Rule 3

The Ultimate Purpose of the Custos' Labors

Let the Custos understand that the ultimate end of all human labor is to provide for his family not temporally but spiritually. As always, the temporal is at the service of the spiritual. Therefore, the Custos' occupation is always at the service of his vocation. His temporal provisions for his family are always at the greater service of feeding his family spiritually. For example, the Custos gathers food to feed his family corporally, and yet the greater end is that the family perceives this food as a gift from God and gives thanks to Him. The Custos labors to provide shelter for his family, and yet the greater end is that his home becomes a domestic church wherein his family experiences prayer, worship, and communion with God.

As the Lord Jesus says, "Do not labor for the food which perishes, but for the food which endures to eternal life, which the Son of man will give to you" (John 6:27). The Lord is not saying that the Custos is not to provide temporally but, rather, that all temporal provisions are at the service of the spiritual. Considering this, the Custos, in all his labors, is working not for himself but for Christ — the Bread that does not perish and the ultimate reason and end of all his labors. Therefore, let him be aware that the three primary purposes of his labors is first, to glorify God; second, to provide spiritually for his domestic church; and third, to provide for the corporal needs of his family. All other motivations for his labors are subject to these three.

Spiritual Practice

Thank God for Your Employment and Your Ability to Work

Work is not intended to be enjoyable and therefore can be a cause of suffering. Yet being able to work, being employed, and having a steady income are gifts from God. Therefore, as the apostle says, "Give thanks in all circumstances" (1 Thess. 5:18).

When confronted with the arduous reality of work, instead of grumbling and complaining, identify the good aspects of your work, such as income, your health, and your ability to think and labor. Then give thanks to God. This is most pleasing to God, as the psalmist says: "Offer to God a sacrifice of thanksgiving" (Ps. 50:14).

Rule 4

The Temptation to Work for Sinful Mammon

Let the Custos be aware that though money is necessary in his efforts to provide for his family, the evil spirits will occasionally instill in him the fear that God will not provide, or that God will not provide enough, in order to convince the Custos to use the means of immoral work to procure the good end of provision for his family. He may be tempted to believe that certain types of employment that would compromise his morality, conflict with his primary vocation, or steal time owed to his family are to his financial advantage. Yet the holy apostle warns, "The love of money is the root of all evils" (1 Tim. 6:10); and our Lord Jesus admonishes, "What does it profit a man, to gain the whole world and forfeit his life?" (Mark 8:36). According to the *Catechism of the Catholic Church*, quoting the Angelic Doctor, "'an evil action cannot be justified by reference to a good intention.' … The end does not justify the means."[13] Therefore, if the Custos' employment involves immoral choices or immoral actions, let him seek employment elsewhere; and if evil mammon is offered to him in exchange for his labors, let him refuse it and seek proper work that glorifies God.

[13] *Catechism of the Catholic Church*, no. 1759, quoting St. Thomas Aquinas, *Dec. praec.* 6.

Spiritual Practice

Do a Moral Inventory of Your Job

Assess your employment and determine whether it is moral and ethical. If not, begin planning an exit strategy without exposing your family to a lack of provision. Be prudent in your efforts to find new employment.

Additionally, you might have a morally ethical job per se but in an environment that your coworkers have conditioned to be immoral and toxic. If those influences begin to compromise your fidelity to and zeal for God, you ought to consider finding new employment.

Rule 5

How the Evil Spirits Will Condition the Custos to Believe That His Work Is His Identity

Let the Custos be aware that the evil spirits will condition him to believe that his identity — that is, who he is — is defined ultimately by his work. Signs that the Custos is surrendering to the grave temptation of deriving his identity from his work are these:

1. He prioritizes the importance of his work above his family or above God (especially by engaging in servile labor on the Lord's Day), or both.
2. He habitually sacrifices time that is allocated for his family in exchange for working beyond the normal workday.
3. He becomes depressed or saddened by his performance at work or by a lack of recognition for his labors.
4. He is elated with pride and inflated with self-confidence due to his achievements at work.
5. While he is with his family, he is continually distracted by his work or is pulled away from his family to tend to his work.

These are certain signs that the Custos' work is becoming an idol, for he is placing more faith in his own labors than in God's providence. As the holy apostle says, "The love of money is the root of all evils; it is through this craving that some have wandered away from the faith and pierced their hearts with many pangs" (1 Tim. 6:10). Therefore, let the Custos find his identity in Christ, as a son in the Son, as a father who reflects the image of God the Father, as a husband who transmits the fidelity and love of the Divine Bridegroom; and let his work support this noble call.

Spiritual Practice

Turn Off Your Work

As previously advised, prior to morning prayer, after evening prayer, and during family evening time, suspend all work and communication with coworkers and collaborators.

Rule 6

Keeping Holy the Lord's Day

Let the Custos understand that the spirit of the Lord's Day is not merely to abstain from work but to keep the day holy — that is, to set it aside for God and His designs and purposes. Therefore, let the Custos be intentional about using the Lord's Day to rest in God, allocating time for prayer and for worship in the Holy Sacrifice of the Mass, to spend time socializing with family and to pray with his family, to serve the less fortunate, and to host those who have none to host them. The spirit of the Day of the Lord is not rigid abstinence from work but, rather, a spirit of charity to God, family, friends, and the less fortunate. Let the Custos understand that he is to have dominion over his work, rather than letting his work have dominion over him, and that by giving God Sunday, God will reward him in his labors throughout the remaining week.

Spiritual Practice

Refrain from Work and Selfish Ambitions on Sunday

On Sunday, refrain from servile labor, house projects, and those activities that distract or distance a man from making the Lord's Day holy. First, commit yourself to giving God the first day of the week (Sunday) as your tithe of time. Resist the temptation to make excuses for your selfishness. Creatively establish ways to use the day for worship, assisting others in need, and celebrating with family and friends.

Rule 7

How the Evil Spirits Will Tempt the Custos to Misuse the Lord's Day for Himself

Let the Custos be aware that the evil spirits will attempt to lure and entice him to work on the Lord's Day or to use it to fulfill his own pursuits, by instilling in him the fear that he is falling behind in his work, that he needs to get ahead on his work, or that he does not have enough time during the week to complete his work or by suggesting that he enjoys his work and therefore it is really not labor. Yet all these reasonings are rooted in fear and selfishness, rather than in trust in God the Father and His providence. As the holy apostle says, "Perfect love casts out fear" (1 John 4:18). As the holy prophet admonishes, "If you turn back your foot from the sabbath, from doing your pleasure on my holy day, and call the sabbath a delight and the holy day of the Lord honorable; if you honor it, not going your own ways, or seeking your own pleasure, or talking idly; then you shall take delight in the Lord, and I will make you ride upon the heights of the earth; I will feed you with the heritage of Jacob your father, for the mouth of the Lord has spoken" (Isa. 58:13–14). Therefore, let the Custos not believe that the sabbath rest is a burden; rather, let him delight in God and honor Him with that day, and the Lord will delight in him and surely bless him. Let the Custos be aware that the more he carries out his own pursuits on the Lord's Day, the less he gives to God; and the more he takes delight in the Lord and finds rest in the Lord on His day, the more he gives to God, and eventually the Lord will bless His labors all the more; for the Lord cannot be outdone in generosity. Keeping holy the sabbath while refraining from fulfilling one's own pursuits is a true mark of divine sonship. This trust in God the Father is a sign that the Lord delights in His son.

Spiritual Practice

Holy Hour

One way to ensure that you are sanctifying or consecrating the Lord's Day to God is by visiting the Lord Jesus in the Most Blessed Sacrament of the Altar. Give to God a Holy Hour or a Holy Half Hour. Identify the time in which you can offer your Holy Hour, and then be consistent. During the time, allow God simply to infuse you with His Holy Presence.

Conclusion

My brother, society goes by way of the family, and the family goes by way of the father. If the world is to be converted, the Church must be renewed. If the universal Church is to be renewed, the domestic church, which makes up the Church, must be restored. If the domestic church is to be restored, marriages must be revitalized. If marriages are to be revitalized, the man who is husband, father, son of God, and spiritual leader must become like St. Joseph, a father on earth like the Father in Heaven.

At the heart of God's plan to save and sanctify souls are the human family and marriage. Sr. Lucia dos Santos, one of the seers at Fátima, is often quoted as saying that the last battle between God and Satan will be over the family and marriage. We are living amid the catastrophic consequences and casualties of this epic confrontation.

The human father stands at the epicenter of this cosmic battle. Two millennia ago, a father, by means of embracing his identity, role, and responsibility, became the savior of the Savior, the master of the Master, the king of the King of Kings, one who fed bread to the Bread of Life. St. Joseph, by establishing in his life the four pillars of embracing silence, embracing woman, embracing the child, and embracing his charitable authority, literally saved the world by protecting and providing for the Christ Child and His Most Holy Mother.

It has often been asked, "What can one man do?" St. Joseph demonstrates that the humble and hidden, silent and strong, gentle and generous father, by establishing St. Joseph's four pillars in his own life, can become the sacrificial saint who can change the course of history and lead souls to the glory of the eternal kingdom.

It is my prayer that, by living St. Joseph's spirituality, you will become like him by doing what he has done, by becoming a father on earth like the Father in Heaven.

Let us turn to St. Joseph often, entrusting ourselves to him so that we may belong completely to the triune God.

Consecration Prayer to St. Joseph

O St. Joseph, predestined and chosen by God from among men, you received the glorious honor of being the chaste guardian of the Most Blessed Virgin Mary. Enflamed with divine love, you received her as your beloved wife, and through her, God bestowed upon you the most privileged distinction of being the virginal father of God the Son.

As a living reflection of the Heavenly Father, you protected the Christ Child from Herod, thus becoming the savior of the Savior. You accepted Jesus' humble submission to your fatherly authority and thus became the master of the Master. As a hidden king, you conferred upon Jesus the Davidic kingship and thus became the king of the King of Kings. With untiring joy, you labored to nurture the human soul and flesh of Jesus, giving bread to the Bread of Life.

Most gentle and generous father, look upon me, your indigent child, and see that I, too, need your care and protection. O chaste heart that burned with love for Jesus and

Mary, teach me, your humble servant, to be devoted entirely to Mary and to worship the Lord Jesus with my entire being that I, too, may become a living reflection of God our Father.

O master of the interior life, you faithfully and promptly fulfilled the divine commands. Your humble obedience has elevated the vocation of fatherhood as a certain means to sublime sanctity and eternal glory. Desiring to follow your holy example, I embrace my vocation to be a most chaste husband, a living icon of God the Father, and a just guardian and guide so that my family may become like yours, a holy family.

Therefore, most glorious and humble spiritual father, today, before the heavenly host, I surrender myself, my marriage, my fatherhood, my family, my labors, my merits, all that I am and have, unreservedly and totally to you and, consequently, to Mary my Queen and most holy Mother, that you may always be my parents in the order of grace and that I may forever be your son.

As you and Mary consecrated the Son of God to God the Father, consecrate me also, so that I may be set apart for holy service to God Most High. I beseech you, as you prepared Christ for His ultimate sacrifice, prepare me also that I may attain the fullness of divine sonship.

Most humble, silent, and hidden father, I surrender all to you so that my fatherhood may glorify God the Father of glory in this age and the age to come, forever without end. Amen.

Appendix 1

Litany of St. Joseph

Lord, have mercy on us.
Lord, have mercy on us.
Christ, have mercy on us.
Christ, have mercy on us.
Lord, have mercy on us.
Lord, have mercy on us.
Christ, hear us.
Christ, graciously hear us.

God the Father of heaven, have mercy on us.
God the Son, Redeemer of the World, have mercy on us.
God the Holy Spirit, have mercy on us.
Holy Trinity, one God, have mercy on us.

Holy Mary, pray for us.
St. Joseph, pray for us.
Renowned offspring of David, pray for us.
Light of Patriarchs, pray for us.
Spouse of the Mother of God, pray for us.
Guardian of the Redeemer, pray for us.

Chaste guardian of the Virgin, pray for us.
Foster father of the Son of God, pray for us.
Diligent protector of Christ, pray for us.
Servant of Christ, pray for us.
Minister of salvation, pray for us.
Head of the Holy Family, pray for us.
Joseph most just, pray for us.
Joseph most chaste, pray for us.
Joseph most prudent, pray for us.
Joseph most strong, pray for us.
Joseph most obedient, pray for us.
Joseph most faithful, pray for us.
Mirror of patience, pray for us.
Lover of poverty, pray for us.
Model of workers, pray for us.
Glory of family life, pray for us.
Guardian of virgins, pray for us.
Pillar of families, pray for us.
Support in difficulties, pray for us.
Solace of the wretched, pray for us.
Hope of the sick, pray for us.
Patron of exiles, pray for us.
Patron of the afflicted, pray for us.
Patron of the poor, pray for us.
Patron of the dying, pray for us.
Terror of demons, pray for us.
Protector of Holy Church, pray for us.

Lamb of God, who takes away the sins of the world,
spare us, O Jesus.
Lamb of God, who takes away the sins of the world,
graciously hear us, O Jesus.
Lamb of God, who takes away the sins of the world,
have mercy on us, O Jesus.

He made him the lord of his household
And prince over all his possessions.

Let us pray: O God, in Your ineffable providence, You were pleased to choose Blessed Joseph to be the spouse of Your most holy Mother; grant, we beg you, that we may be worthy to have him for our intercessor in Heaven whom on earth we venerate as our Protector: You who live and reign forever and ever.

Saint Joseph, pray for us.

Appendix 2

Daily Examination of Conscience

Toward the end of the day, prior to retiring for the evening or before getting into bed, take a couple of moments to examine your conscience. To do this, assume a prayerful position, such as kneeling or lying prostrate, and invoke the Holy Spirit to help you examine your thoughts, words, and actions throughout the day. This does not need to be an exacting process. Ideally, first recount the blessings of the day and give God thanks for them. Second, reflect upon and confess to God your thoughts, words, and actions that were not in conformity with His holy will or are sinful. Third, after acknowledging your sins, make a heartfelt act of contrition, asking God for His mercy and forgiveness and the grace necessary to avoid the near occasions of sin in the future.

The Ten Commandments can be used as a guide in examining your conscience, but sometimes these commandments may be too broad and general. Another powerful way to examine yourself is by using Christ's Beatitudes:

- *Blessed are the poor in Spirit* (Matt. 5:3): Was I prideful, self-seeking, self-glorifying, self-important, placing myself above others today? Have I responded to the people and circumstances in my life with humility, accepting them as though they are from God?

- *Blessed are those who mourn* (Matt. 5:4): Do I have true sorrow and contrition for my sins? Have I repented and done penance for my past sins? Do I seriously consider that my sins of the past may have led individuals to sin against God, perhaps even damnation? Do I ask God to make right my wrongs and redeem my omissions? Do I consider that it was for my sins that the Son of God was tortured and gave His life?
- *Blessed are the meek* (Matt. 5:5): Did I allow anger to be the driving force behind my actions? Did I vent my anger, raise my voice, and act in a demeaning way toward those around me? Do I allow Church politics, government politics, family situations, or obstacles at work or at home to arouse my anger? Or do I give such situations to God and allow the Holy Spirit to help me deal with them rationally and calmly?
- *Blessed are those who hunger and thirst for righteousness* (Matt. 5:6): Do I desire the right over the wrong, the moral over the immoral? Do I rejoice when evil or immorality is lauded? Do I approve of videos, movies, posts, and tweets that contain illicit or immoral messages? Do I share such things or find humor in them? Am I fair in my dealings with others, particularly in business and finances? Have I stolen anyone's goods, content, or good reputation? If so, have I made amends? Justice is seeking God first and giving Him His due: Do I seek God first in all matters? Do I give God the firstfruits of my money and time?
- *Blessed are the merciful* (Matt. 5:7): Have I refused to forgive someone who has offended me? Have I sought forgiveness

from someone I have offended or sinned against? Have I judged, condemned, or criticized another unjustly? Have I judged another without considering my own wretchedness, failings, and sins?

- *Blessed are the pure in heart* (Matt. 5:8): Do I view the human body as an object of desire, to be used for my disordered gratification? Do I use pornography in any form? Do I avoid ads, posts, or news feeds that display people in sexually provocative situations? Do I make every attempt to see a woman as an equal, with equal dignity, or do I reduce her to her bodily attributes? Do I use or manipulate people to obtain what I desire from them? Or do I love my neighbors for who they are, without expecting anything in return? Have I been jealous or envious of another person or of that person's status, talents, gifts, or possessions? Do I praise God for His glory in others, even when I don't possess that particular glory?
- *Blessed are the peacemakers for they shall be called sons of God* (Matt. 5:9): Are there any persons whom I have needlessly offended, insulted, and displayed a lack of charity toward? Are any of my relationships (with my wife, children, relatives, friends, coworkers) strained, and do they necessitate an attempt toward reconciliation? Is there anyone who has injured me whom I have not forgiven? Is there anyone I have injured from whom I need to ask for forgiveness? Do I have any debts for which I have not made just restitution?
- *Blessed are those who suffer persecution for justice and for Christ's sake* (see Matt. 5:10–11): Am I ashamed to share or display my belief in Jesus Christ? Am I afraid to pray in

public? Do I avoid discussing my faith with others? Do I avoid or neglect protecting another's good actions, just cause, or belief in God because I am afraid of being persecuted?

About the Author

Devin Schadt is the executive director of the Fathers of St. Joseph, an apostolate that labors for the restoration, redemption, and revitalization of fatherhood by helping men live St. Joseph's spirituality. Devin is the author of more than twenty books and is a frequent guest on Relevant Radio and the co-host of *The Catholic Gentleman*. He posts weekly on *The Way of a Man* blog. Devin lives with his wife and five daughters in the Midwest. Learn more at fathersofstjoseph.org.

Sophia Institute

Sophia Institute is a nonprofit institution that seeks to nurture the spiritual, moral, and cultural life of souls and to spread the gospel of Christ in conformity with the authentic teachings of the Roman Catholic Church.

Sophia Institute Press fulfills this mission by offering translations, reprints, and new publications that afford readers a rich source of the enduring wisdom of mankind.

Sophia Institute also operates the popular online resource CatholicExchange.com. *Catholic Exchange* provides world news from a Catholic perspective as well as daily devotionals and articles that will help readers to grow in holiness and live a life consistent with the teachings of the Church.

In 2013, Sophia Institute launched Sophia Institute for Teachers to renew and rebuild Catholic culture through service to Catholic education. With the goal of nurturing the spiritual, moral, and cultural life of souls, and an abiding respect for the role and work of teachers, we strive to provide materials and programs that are at once enlightening to the mind and ennobling to the heart; faithful and complete, as well as useful and practical.

Sophia Institute gratefully recognizes the Solidarity Association for preserving and encouraging the growth of our apostolate over the course of many years. Without their generous and timely support, this book would not be in your hands.

www.SophiaInstitute.com
www.CatholicExchange.com
www.SophiaInstituteforTeachers.org

Sophia Institute Press® is a registered trademark of Sophia Institute.
Sophia Institute is a tax-exempt institution as defined by the Internal Revenue Code, Section 501(c)(3). Tax ID 22-2548708.